Praise for Jack Canfield and his Success Principles™

Canfield's principles are simple, but the results you'll achieve will be extraordinary!

Anthony Robbins, author of *Awaken the Giant Within* and *Unlimited Power*

If you could only read one book this year, you have it in your hands.

Harvey Mackay, author of the New York Times number one best seller *Swim with the Sharks without Being Eaten Alive*

When Jack Canfield writes, I listen. This is Jack's finest piece of writing and will impact your life forever.

Pat Williams, senior vice president of the NBA's Orlando Magic

Jack Canfield is a Master of his medium, giving people who are hungry for more life the wisdom, insights, understanding, and inspiration they need to achieve it. Great book, great read, great gift for anyone committed to becoming a Master of Life!

Michael E. Gerber, author of The E-Myth books

Canfield and Switzer have put their methods to success in an illuminating and easy-to-read book. Jack's teaching is highly effective and this new book will be the gift to give this year.

Ken Blanchard, coauthor of *The One M* and *Customer Mania!*®

Jack's message is simple, powerful, and practical. If you work the principles, the principles work. A must-read for those who want to create the successful life about which they dream.

Andrew Puzder, president and CEO of CKE Restaurants, Inc., Carl's Jr., Hardee's, and La Salsa

Page for page the best system for achieving anything you want. Get ready for the ride of your life. I couldn't put it down!

Marcia Martin, former vice president of EST and transformational coach

My good friend Jack Canfield is one of the most insightful speakers and teachers in the world today. After you have spent time with him, internalizing his ideas and insights, you will be changed in a positive way for the rest of your life.

Brian Tracy, one of America's leading authorities on the development of human potential and personal effectiveness and author of *Success Is a Journey*, *Million Dollar Habits*, and *The Traits of Champions*

What a great collection of "successful" thoughts and ideas … some simple, some profound, and all "essential" in today's complex world … a must-read!

Steven Stralser, Ph.D., managing director of and clinical professor at the Global Entrepreneurship Center, Thunderbird: The Garvin School of International Management, and author of *MBA in a Day: What You Would Learn in Top-Tier Schools of Business – If You Only Had the Time*

If you've ever wanted Jack Canfield to personally mentor you in achieving your highest vision, this book is the next best thing to having him as your personal guide. It's packed with information, inspiration, and – most importantly – understanding. Along with his proven strategies, Jack's support, compassion, and integrity shine through.

Marshall Thurber, cofounder of the Accelerated Business School and Money and You

The success principles in this book are so simple to follow but at the same time so powerful. They are essential to achieving your goals. Jack has a way of making learning entertaining and fun. This book is a true winner!

Kathy Coover, cofounder and senior VP of sales and marketing of Isagenix International

This book is a brilliantly written, masterful distillation of the leading principles and processes available today for creating real success in your life.

Hale Dwoskin, author of the New York Times best seller *The Sedona Method: Your Key to Lasting Happiness, Success, Peace, and Emotional Well-being*

I used the principles in this book to propel my Web site from 100 visitors a month to over 5,000 visitors a month.

Zev Saftlas, author of *Motivation That Works* and founder of empoweringmessages.com

Canfield and Switzer have created a book that is alive with intellect, compassion, and humor. This is one of the best books on success I have ever read! If you have a dream that you have not yet attained, let Jack Canfield lead the way. You will be happy you did.

Bill Cirone, superintendent of Santa Barbara County Office of Education

If you're looking for a winning plan for success, look no further than Jack Canfield's Success Principles.

Suzanne de Passe, television producer

I have been a student of Jack Canfield for over a decade and have used the principles he teaches in this book to accelerate my own success and the success of the people I train and manage at the Henry Ford Museum. This book has my highest recommendation. It will change your life.

Jim Van Bochove, director of workforce development at The Henry Ford: America's Greatest History Attraction

Jack Canfield's Success Principles brilliantly and succinctly imparts the tried and true formula for living a successful, fulfilled life. You will find inspiration and motivation on every page.

Debbie Ford, number one New York Times best-selling author of *The Dark Side of the Light Chasers* and *The Best Year of Your Life*

Jack Canfield has, with diamond-like clarity, crafted the ultimate success manual. It's the manual I wish I'd had when I began my quest for the best.

Master Mary Louise Zeller, "Ninja Grandma," twelve-time national and five-time international gold medalist in Olympic-style tae kwon do

How to Get from Where You Are to Where You Want to Be

THE 25 PRINCIPLES OF SUCCESS

Jack Canfield

HarperElement
An Imprint of HarperCollins*Publishers*
77–85 Fulham Palace Road,
Hammersmith, London W6 8JB

The website address is:
www.thorsonselement.com

and *HarperElement* are trademarks of
HarperCollins*Publishers* Ltd

Adapted from *The Success Principles*,
first published in the US by HarperCollins*Publishers* Ltd 2005
This edition first published 2007

1 3 5 7 9 10 8 6 4 2

© 2005, 2007 Jack Canfield

Jack Canfield asserts the moral right to
be identified as the author of this work

A catalogue record of this book
is available from the British Library

ISBN-13 978-0-00-724575-8
ISBN-10 0-00-724575-0

Printed and bound in Great Britain by
Clays Ltd, St Ives plc

All rights reserved. No part of this publication may be
reproduced, stored in a retrieval system, or transmitted,
in any form or by any means, electronic, mechanical,
photocopying, recording or otherwise, without the prior
written permission of the publishers.

This book is proudly printed on paper which contains wood
from well managed forests, certified in accordance with
the rules of the Forest Stewardship Council.
For more information about FSC,
please visit www.fsc-uk.org

Mixed Sources
Product group from well-managed
forests and other controlled sources
www.fsc.org   Cert no. SW-COC-1806
© 1996 Forest Stewardship Council

FSC

Contents

Acknowledgments   ix

Introduction   xvii

The Success Principles

1. Take 100% Responsibility for Your Life   1
2. Be Clear Why You're Here   28
3. Decide What You Want   37
4. Believe It's Possible   53
5. Believe in Yourself   60
6. Become an Inverse Paranoid   70
7. Unleash the Power of Goal-Setting   79
8. Chunk It Down   97
9. Success Leaves Clues   104
10. Release the Brakes   108
11. See What You Want, Get What You See   125
12. Act As If   141
13. Take Action   154
14. Feel the Fear and Do It Anyway   171
15. Ask! Ask! Ask!   198
16. Reject Rejection   209
17. Use Feedback to Your Advantage   220
18. Commit to Constant and Never-Ending Improvement   239
19. Practice Persistence   245
20. Practice the Rule of Five   256
21. Surround Yourself with Successful People   261

22. Clean Up Your Messes and Your Incompletes   270

23. Develop Four New Success Habits a Year   279

24. Stay Focused on Your Core Genius   285

25. Start Now! ... Just Do It!   292

Notes   305

Suggested Reading and Additional Resources   311

About the Authors   328

Permissions   333

Index   339

Acknowledgments

This book, like everything else I have created in my life, is the result of a huge team effort. I extend my deepest gratitude and thanks to:

Janet Switzer, without whose Herculean efforts this book would never have been completed. Thank you for your incredible support, deep insights, and long days (and nights!) spent in the original conception of this book, coauthoring a world-class book proposal, boiling my endless production of written words down into a manageable manuscript, keeping me focused, developing the Success Principles Web site, and creating such an amazing marketing plan for reaching millions of people with the message of this book. You are truly awesome!

Bonnie Solow, my literary agent. You are more than an agent. You were there every step of the way with your editorial insights, emotional support, enthusiastic encouragement, and authentic friendship. I admire your integrity, your professionalism, your commitment to excellence, your sincere desire to make a difference, and your love for life.

Steve Hanselman, my brilliant, supportive, and insightful editor and publisher at HarperCollins. Thanks for your boundless energy, your beautiful spirit, and your dedication to educating and uplifting humanity through the written word.

Jane Friedman, president and CEO of HarperCollins, who championed this book from the beginning. Thanks for the inspiring job you do of running a company aligned with the principles described in this book. It is an honor to be working with you.

Katharine O'Moore-Klopf, who copyedited the original manuscript. Your eagle eye and attention to detail are awesome. Thanks for a wonderful job.

Patty Aubery, president of Chicken Soup for the Soul Enterprises, for "making" me write this book. Thanks for overseeing the whole project and especially for helping get all of the endorsements. You are an awesome friend and business partner. Words can never convey how much I appreciate your support in bringing out the best in me.

Russell Kamalski, chief operating officer at Chicken Soup for the Soul Enterprises. Thanks for your calm, easygoing demeanor that helps keep it all together in the midst of the tornado-like frenzy we often find ourselves in. You're a true gentleman.

Veronica Romero, my executive assistant, who has kept my life in order with very little support from me during the last year of being buried under the weight of this project. Thanks for scheduling all of the interviews and for overseeing getting all of the necessary permissions for this book. Thanks for keeping me, my travel, and my speaking career alive and well during this time. Your tireless efforts, your attention to detail, and your commitment to excellence are awesome. Thanks so much!

Mike Foster, my other executive assistant, thanks for your help in keeping the wolves at bay so I could have the space to work on this book with a minimum of interruptions, your research support, your long hours, your sense of humor, and your shared vision. Your commitment above and beyond the call of duty to keeping our seminars filled and our computers working is also awesome. Thanks for your dedication and your love.

Jesse Ianniello, for all of her endless hours of transcribing the hundreds of hours of interviews I recorded, and for all of the other endless clerical tasks that were required to complete this book. You consistently make the difficult look easy. You are a wonder.

Robin Yerian, for looking after me in so many areas of my life, especially making sure we stay on budget so that we always have enough money to do the things we need to do.

Teresa Esparza, for managing to coordinate all my speaking engagements and keeping all of our clients happy during this "year of the book." D'ette Corona for brilliantly overseeing the *Chicken Soup for the Soul®* production schedule while I was diverted by this project. You, too, are awesome!

Heather McNamara, Nancy Mitchell Autio, Leslie Riskin, Stephanie Thatcher, Barbara Lomonaco, and Tasha Boucher, who handled all of the details of getting *Chicken Soup* books completed and out the door during this time. And all the other people who work at Self-Esteem Seminars and Chicken Soup for the Soul Enterprises.

Erick Baldwin, Kristen Craib, Lauren Edelstein, Devon Foster, Anna Giardina, Chris Muirhead, and Danielle Schlapper, our fabulous interns from the University of California, Santa Barbara, for your typing, editing and research skills.

Gail Miller, Janet's director of training programs, who manages Janet's company so brilliantly and who continually creates the space Janet needs to help develop The Success Principles book and training products. Your intelligence and the results you produce are truly impressive.

Rick Frischman, David Hahn, and Jared Sharpe at Planned Television Arts for their world-class support in getting the word out to the folks in radio and television land. I love working with you guys!

Hale Dwoskin, Marshall Thurber, and Barbara De Angelis, for their constant encouragement and offers of support throughout the writing of this book.

The following people who allowed me to interview them, and whose stories and anecdotes appear in this book: Robert Allen, Jeff Arch, John Assaraf, Stephen J. Cannell, D.C. Cordova, John Demartini, Harv Eker, Tim Ferriss, Ruben Gonzales, Mike Kelley, Marilyn Kentz, Julie Laipply, Dave Liniger, Debbie Macomber, Chad Pregracke, Monty Roberts, Diana Von Welanetz Wentworth, and Pat Williams.

The many other people who allowed me to interview

them, and though because of space constrictions and last-minute editing, their stories don't appear in this book, their ideas, insights, and spirit are woven throughout.

The hundreds of people who offered to be interviewed for the book – you know who you are – but whom I simply couldn't get to because of time, which I regret, because conducting the interviews was the most exciting part of creating this book. This project taught me once again just how much valuable information we all have to share with each other. I hope someday to be able to take all of you up on your offers for a future book.

The following people, who have directly influenced my thinking about and achievement of success in their workshops, seminars, and coaching programs, over the years: W. Clement Stone, Og Mandino, Norman Vincent Peale, Marshall Thurber, Mark Victor Hansen, Phil Laut, Leonard Orr, Stewart Emery, Martha Crampton, Russell Bishop, Jim Newman, Lou Tice, John Gray, Tim Piering, Tracy Goss, Martin Rutte, Wayne Dyer, Bob Proctor, Lee Pulos, Brian Tracy, Jim Rohn, Anthony Robbins, Michael Gerber, Dan Sullivan, Les Hewitt, Robert Allen, Hale Dwoskin, and John Assaraf. Thanks for your brilliant minds, your courage to live on the cutting edge, and your generosity of spirit.

The members of my mastermind group: John Assaraf, Lee Brower, Declan Dunn, Liz Edlic, and Marshall Thurber. I appreciate being part of such a loving and visionary band of brothers and sisters.

Mark Victor Hansen and Patty Hansen for their love,

friendship, and partnership on the *Chicken Soup for the Soul®* journey, which has been the greatest adventure of my life.

Peter Vegso and Gary Seidler at Health Communications Inc., for believing in the dream long before anyone else did, and without whose support over the years this book would have never been created. Thanks, guys! And everyone else at HCI who has worked to make *Chicken Soup for the Soul®* a worldwide publishing phenomenon.

All my family for their love, support, and understanding during what has been unquestionably the greatest professional challenge of my career. Thanks for understanding the long hours, the sacrificed weekends, and the canceled vacations that were required. I love and appreciate you all so much. Inga, my wife, whom I adore for how much she understands me and what I am about, and for her unceasing love, support, humor, and encouragement. Christopher, my son, and Riley and Travis, my two stepchildren. Thanks for being so supportive. And Oran and Kyle, my two older sons. My sister Kim, for all of her moral support and encouragement when I couldn't see the light at the end of the tunnel. It's nice having a sister who is a fellow writer and understands the process. Taylor and Mary, for taking care of Mom all these many months and years. Rick and Tana, for being such a good brother and sister-in-law. Fred Angelis, my stepfather, for taking me under his wing when I was 6 and providing me with the values and work habits that have allowed me to create the level of success that I have.

Janet's family, for their support, understanding, and good humor in the face of missed vacations and endless book-related dinner conversation. To her parents, Les and Beverly, who showed Janet early on the meaning of success and who fostered an atmosphere of achievement in their home. To her siblings, Jennifer and Jeff, for their constant support and encouragement through every new step in Janet's life and career. And most especially, thanks to Janet's niece Brianne, who not only reflects how children learn to be successful but is also a gentle reminder that the most important thing is to enjoy it.

And finally, thanks to all of the assistants and participants in my seminars and workshops these past few years for sharing their dreams, struggles, and triumphs with me. Your heroic efforts in overcoming your limiting beliefs and fears, your courage in confronting the obstacles in your paths, your perseverance in the face of adversity, and the amazing lives you have all created are the inspiration that led me to write this book and share these principles with others. Thank you for being the models of vision, purpose, and passion that the world so desperately needs. Know that you are all represented in these pages.

This book is dedicated to all those courageous men and women who have ever dared to step out of the dominant culture of resignation and mediocrity and endeavor to create the life of their dreams. I honor and salute you!

Life is like a combination lock; your job is
to find the right numbers, in the right order,
so you can have anything you want.

Brian Tracy

If we did all the things we are capable of doing,
we would literally astound ourselves.

Thomas A. Edison

It's time to start living the life you've imagined.

Henry James

Introduction

If a man for whatever reason has the opportunity
to lead an extraordinary life, he has no right
to keep it to himself.

Jacques-Yves Cousteau – Legendary underwater explorer and filmmaker

If a man writes a book, let him set down only what he
knows. I have guesses enough of my own.

Johann Wolfgang von Goethe – German poet, novelist,
playwright, and philosopher

This is not a book of good ideas. This is a book of timeless
principles used by successful men and women throughout history. I have studied these success principles for
over 30 years and have applied them to my own life. The
phenomenal level of success that I now enjoy is the result
of applying these principles day in and day out since I began to learn them in 1968.

My success includes being the author and editor of over
60 best-selling books with over 100 million copies in print
in 46 languages around the world, holding a Guinness
Book world record for having seven books on the May

24, 1998, *New York Times* bestseller list, earning a multimillion-dollar net income every year for over the past 10 years, living in a beautiful California estate, appearing on every major talk show in America (from *Oprah* to *Good Morning America*), having a weekly newspaper column read by millions every week, commanding speaking fees of $25,000 a talk, speaking to Fortune 500 companies all over the world, being the recipient of numerous professional and civic awards, having an outrageous relationship with my amazing wife and wonderful children, and having achieved a steady state of wellness, balance, happiness, and inner peace.

I get to socialize with CEOs of Fortune 500 companies; movie, television, and recording stars; celebrated authors; and the world's finest spiritual teachers and leaders. I have spoken to the members of Congress, professional athletes, corporate managers, and sales superstars in all of the best resorts and retreat centers of the world – from the Four Seasons Resort in Nevis in the West Indies to the finest hotels in Acapulco and Cancun. I get to ski in Idaho, California, and Utah, go rafting in Colorado, and hike in the mountains of California and Washington. And I get to vacation in the world's best resorts in Hawaii, Australia, Thailand, Morocco, France, and Italy. All in all, life is a real kick!

And like most of you reading this book, my life started out in a very average way. I grew up in Wheeling, West Virginia, where my dad worked in a florist's shop, where he made $8,000 a year. My mother was an alcoholic and my father was a workaholic. I worked during the summers to make ends meet (as a lifeguard at a pool and at the same florist's shop as my father). I went to college on a scholarship and held a job serving breakfast in one of the dorms to pay for books, clothes, and dates. Nobody handed me anything on a silver platter. During my last year of graduate school, I had a part-time teaching job that paid me $120 every 2 weeks. My rent was $79 a month, so that left $161 to cover all my other expenses. Toward the end of the month, I ate what became known as my 21-cent dinners – a 10-cent can of tomato paste, garlic salt, and water over an 11-cent bag of spaghetti noodles. I know what it is like to be scraping by on the bottom rungs of the economic ladder.

After graduate school, I started my career as a high school history teacher in an all-black school on the south side of Chicago. And then I met my mentor, W. Clement Stone. Stone was a self-made multimillionaire who hired me to work in his foundation, where he trained me in the fundamental success principles that I still operate from today. My job was to teach these same principles to others. Over the years, I have gone on from my time with Stone to interview hundreds of successful people – Olympic and professional athletes, celebrated entertainers, best-selling authors, business leaders, political leaders, successful entrepreneurs, and top salespeople. I have read literally thousands of books (I average one every 2 days), attended hundreds of seminars, and listened to thousands of hours of audio programs to uncover the universal principles for creating success and happiness. I then applied those principles to my own life. The ones that worked I have taught in my speeches, seminars, and workshops to well over 1 million people in all 50 U.S. states . . . and in 20 countries around the world.

These principles and techniques have not only worked for me but they have also helped hundreds of thousands of my students achieve breakthrough success in their careers, greater wealth in their finances, greater aliveness and joy in their relationships, and greater happiness and fulfillment in their lives. My students have started successful businesses, become self-made millionaires, achieved athletic stardom, received lucrative recording contracts, starred in movie and television roles, won political offices, had huge impact in their communities, written best-selling books, been named teacher of the year in their school districts, broken all the sales records in their companies, written award-winning screenplays, become presidents of their corporations, been recognized for their outstanding philanthropic contributions, created highly successful relationships, and raised unusually happy and successful children.

The Principles Always Work if You Work the Principles

All of these same results are also possible for you. I know for a fact that you, too, can attain unimagined levels of success. Why? Because the principles and techniques always work – all you have to do is put them to work for you.

A few years ago, I was on a television show in Dallas, Texas. I had made the claim that if people would use the principles I was teaching, they could double their income and double their time off in less than 2 years. The woman interviewing me was highly skeptical. I told her that if she used the principles and techniques for 2 years and she didn't double her income and double her time off, I would come back on her show and write her a check for $1,000. If they did work, she had to ask me back and tell her viewers the principles had worked. A short 9 months later, I ran into her at the National Speakers Association convention in Orlando, Florida. She told me that not only had she *already* doubled her income but she had also moved to a bigger station with a substantial pay increase, had started a public speaking career, and had already finished and sold a book – all in just 9 months!

The fact is that anyone can consistently produce these kinds of results on a regular basis. All you have to do is decide what it is you want, believe you deserve it, and practice the success principles in this book.

The fundamentals are the same for all people and all

professions – even if you're currently unemployed. It doesn't matter if your goals are to be the top salesperson in your company, become a leading architect, get all A's in school, lose weight, buy your dream home, or become a world-class professional athlete, a rock star, an award-winning journalist, a multimillionaire, or a successful entrepreneur – the principles and strategies are the same. And if you learn them, assimilate them, and apply them with discipline every day, they will transform your life beyond your wildest dreams.

"You Can't Hire Someone Else to Do Your Push-Ups for You"

As motivational philosopher Jim Rohn has so aptly put it, "You can't hire someone else to do your push-ups for you." You must do them yourself if you are to get any value out of them. Whether it is exercising, stretching, meditating, reading, studying, learning a new language, creating a mastermind group, setting measurable goals, visualizing success, repeating affirmations, or practicing a new skill, *you* are going to have to do it. No one else can do these things for you. I will give you the road map, but you will have to drive the car. I will teach you the principles, but you will have to apply them. If you choose to put in the effort, I promise you the rewards will be well worth it.

How This Book Is Structured

To help you quickly learn these powerful Principles, you'll start by exploring the absolute necessity of taking 100% responsibility for your life and your results. From there, you'll learn how to clarify your life purpose, your vision, and what you truly want. Next we'll look at how to create an unshakable belief in yourself and your dreams. Then I'll help you turn your vision into a set of concrete goals and an action plan for achieving them. I'll even teach you how to harness the incredible power of affirmations and visualization – one of the success secrets of all Olympic athletes, top entrepreneurs, world leaders, and others.

The next few Principles have to do with taking those necessary but sometimes scary action steps that are required to make your dreams come true. You'll learn to ask for what you want, reject rejection, solicit and respond to feedback, and persevere in the face of what can sometimes seem like insurmountable obstacles. Next you'll learn how to surround yourself with successful people and we'll look at how to clean up any physical and emotional messes you have created and complete all the "incompletes" in your life robbing you of valuable energy that could be better used in the achievement of your goals. I'll also teach you how to develop valuable success habits that will change your life forever, and the importance of spending time focusing exclusively on your core genius. The final Principle focuses on the importance of getting started now!

Together, these 25 Success Principles will jump-start you in creating the life you've always dreamed of but up until now may not have fully known how to create.

How to Read This Book

> Believe nothing. No matter where you read it, or who said it, even if I have said it, unless it agrees with your own reason and your own common sense.
>
> **Buddha**

Everyone learns differently, and you probably know how you learn best. And though there are many ways that you can read this book, I'd like to make a few suggestions that may be helpful.

You may want to read this book through once just to get a feel for the total process before you start the work of creating the life you truly want. The principles are presented in an order that builds one upon the other. They are like the numbers in a combination lock – you need all the numbers, and you need them in the right order. It doesn't matter what color, race, gender, or age you are. If you know the combination, the lock has to open for you.

As you are reading, I strongly encourage you to underline and highlight everything that feels important to you. Make notes in the margin about the things you'll put into action. Then review those notes and highlighted sections again and again. Repetition is the key to real learning. Every time you reread portions of this book, you'll literally "re-mind" yourself of what you need to do to get from where you are to where you want to be. As you'll discover, it takes repetitive exposure to a new idea before it becomes a natural part of your way of thinking and being.

You may also discover that you're already familiar with some of the principles here. That's great! But ask yourself, *Am I currently practicing them?* If not, make a commitment to put them into action – now!

Remember, the Principles only work if you work the Principles.

A Warning

Of course, any change requires sustained effort to overcome years' worth of internal and external resistance. Initially you may find yourself getting very excited about all this new information. You may feel a newfound sense of hope and enthusiasm for the new vision of your life as it can be. This is good. But be forewarned that you may also begin to experience other feelings as well. You may feel frustration at not knowing about all of this earlier, anger at your parents and teachers for not teaching you these important concepts at home and at school, or anger at yourself for having already learned many of these things and not having acted on them.

Just take a deep breath and realize that this is all part of the process of your journey. Everything in the past has actually been perfect. Everything in your past has led you to this transformative moment in time. Everyone – including you – has always done the best they could with what they knew at the time. Now you are about to know more. Celebrate your new awareness! It is about to set you free.

You may also find that there will be times when you wonder, *Why isn't all of this working faster? Why haven't I already achieved my goal? Why aren't I rich already? Why don't I have the man or woman of my dreams by now? When am I going to achieve my ideal weight?* Success takes time, effort, perseverance, and patience. If you apply all of the principles and techniques covered in this book you will achieve your goals. You will realize your dreams. But it won't happen overnight.

It's natural in the achievement of any goal to come upon obstacles, to feel temporarily stuck on a plateau. This is normal. Anyone who has ever played a musical instrument, participated in a sport, or practiced a martial art knows that you hit plateaus where it seems as if you are making no progress whatsoever. That's when the uninitiated often quit, give up, drop out, or take up another instrument or sport. But the wise have discovered if they just keep practicing their instrument, sport, or martial art (or, in your case, the success principles in this book), eventually they make what feels like a sudden leap to a higher level of proficiency. Be patient. Hang in there. Don't give up. You *will* break through. The principles *always* work.

Okay, let's get started.

Principle 1

Take 100% Responsibility for Your Life

You must take personal responsibility.
You cannot change the circumstances, the seasons,
or the wind, but you can change yourself.

Jim Rohn – America's foremost business philosopher

One of the most pervasive myths in the American culture today is that we are *entitled* to a great life – that somehow, somewhere, someone (certainly not us) is responsible for filling our lives with continual happiness, exciting career options, nurturing family time, and blissful personal relationships simply because we exist.

But the real truth – and the one lesson this whole book is based on – is that there is only one person responsible for the quality of the life you live.

That person is *you*.

If you want to be successful, you have to take 100% responsibility for everything that you experience in your life. This includes the level of your achievements, the results you produce, the quality of your relationships, the state of your health and physical fitness, your income, your debts, your feelings – everything!

This is not easy.

In fact, most of us have been conditioned to blame something outside of ourselves for the parts of our life we don't like. We blame our parents, our bosses, our friends, the media, our coworkers, our clients, our spouse, the weather, the economy, our astrological chart, our lack of money – anyone or anything we can pin the blame on. We never want to look at where the real problem is – ourselves.

There is a wonderful story told about a man who is out walking one night and comes upon another man down on his knees looking for something under a streetlamp. The passerby inquires as to what the other man is looking for. He answers that he is looking for his lost key. The passer-by offers to help and gets down on his knees and helps him search for the key. After an hour of fruitless searching, he says, "We've looked everywhere for it and we haven't found it. Are you sure that you lost it here?"

The other man replies, "No, I lost it in my house, but there is more light out here under the streetlamp."

It is time to stop looking outside yourself for the an-swers to why you haven't created the life and results you want, for it is you who creates the quality of the life you lead and the results you produce.

You – no one else!

To achieve major success in life – to achieve those things that are most important to you – you must assume 100% responsibility for your life. Nothing less will do.

100% Responsibility for Everything

As I mentioned in the introduction, back in 1969 – only 1 year out of graduate school – I had the good fortune to work for W. Clement Stone. He was a self-made multi-millionaire worth $600 million at the time – and that was long before all the dot-com millionaires came along in the '90s. Stone was also America's premier success guru. He was the publisher of *Success Magazine*, author of *The Success System That Never Fails*, and coauthor with Napoleon Hill of *Success Through a Positive Mental Attitude*.

When I was completing my first week's orientation, Mr. Stone asked me if I took 100% responsibility for my life.

"I think so," I responded.

"This is a yes or no question, young man. You either do or you don't."

"Well, I guess I'm not sure."

"Have you ever blamed anyone for any circumstance in your life? Have you ever complained about anything?"

"Uh ... yeah ... I guess I have."

"Don't guess. Think."

"Yes, I have."

"Okay, then. That means you don't take 100% responsibility for your life. Taking 100% responsibility means you acknowledge that you create everything that happens to you. It means you understand that you are the cause of all of your experience. If you want to be really successful, and I know you do, then you will have to give up blaming and complaining and take total responsibility for your life – that means all your results, both your successes and your failures. That is the prerequisite for creating a life of success. It is only by acknowledging that you have created everything up until now that you can take charge of creating the future you want.

"You see, Jack, if you realize that you have created your current conditions, then you can uncreate them and re-create them at will. Do you understand that?"

"Yes, sir, I do."

"Are you willing to take 100% responsibility for your life?"

"Yes, sir, I am!"

And I did.

You Have to Give Up All Your Excuses

99% of all failures come from people who have a habit of making excuses.

George Washington Carver
Chemist who discovered over 325 uses for the peanut

If you want to create the life of your dreams, then you are going to have to take 100% responsibility for your life as well. That means giving up all your excuses, all your victim stories, all the reasons why you can't and why you haven't up until now, and all your blaming of outside circumstances. You have to give them all up forever.

You have to take the position that you have always had the power to make it different, to get it right, to produce the desired result. For whatever reason – ignorance, lack of awareness, fear, needing to be right, the need to feel safe – you chose not to exercise that power. Who knows why? It doesn't matter. The past is the past. All that matters now is that from this point forward you choose – that's right, it's a choice – you choose to act as if (that's all that's required – to act as if) you are 100% responsible for everything that does or doesn't happen to you.

If something doesn't turn out as planned, you will ask yourself, "How did I create that? What was I thinking? What were my beliefs? What did I say or not say? What did I do or not do to create that result? How did I get the other person to act that way? What do I need to do differently next time to get the result I want?"

A few years after I met Mr. Stone, Dr. Robert Resnick, a psychotherapist in Los Angeles, taught me a very simple but very important formula that made this idea of 100% responsibility even clearer to me. The formula is:

E + R = O
(Event + Response = Outcome)

The basic idea is that every outcome you experience in life (whether it is success or failure, wealth or poverty, health or illness, intimacy or estrangement, joy or frustration) is the result of how you have responded to an earlier event or events in your life.

If you don't like the outcomes you are currently getting, there are two basic choices you can make.

1. **You can blame the event (E) for your lack of results (O).** In other words, you can blame the economy, the weather, the lack of money, your lack of education, racism, gender bias, the current administration in Washington, your wife or husband, your boss's attitude, the lack of support, the political climate, the system or lack of systems, and so on. If you're a golfer, you've probably even blamed your clubs and the course you played on. No doubt all these factors do exist, but if they were *the* deciding factor, nobody would ever succeed.

Jackie Robinson would never have played major league baseball, Sidney Poitier and Denzel Washington would have never become movie stars, Dianne Feinstein and Barbara Boxer would never have become U.S. senators, Erin Brockovich would never have uncovered PG&E's contamination of the water in Hinkley, California, Bill Gates would never have founded Microsoft, and Steve Jobs would never have started Apple Computers. For every reason why it's not possible, there are hundreds of people who have faced the same circumstances and succeeded.

Lots of people overcome these so-called limiting factors, so it can't be the limiting factors that limit you. It is not the external conditions and circumstances that stop you – it is you! We stop ourselves! We think limiting thoughts and engage in self-defeating behaviors. We defend our self-destructive habits (such as drinking and smoking) with indefensible logic. We ignore useful feedback, fail to continuously educate ourselves and learn new skills, waste time on the trivial aspects of our lives, engage in idle gossip, eat unhealthy food, fail to exercise, spend more money than we make, fail to invest in our future, avoid necessary conflict, fail to tell the truth, don't ask for what we want – and then wonder why our lives don't work. But this, by the way, is what most people do. They place the blame for everything that isn't the way they want it on outside events and circumstances. They have an excuse for everything.

2. **You can instead simply change your responses (R) to the events (E) – the way things are – until you get the outcomes (O) you want.** You can change your thinking, change your communication, change the pictures you hold in your head (your images of yourself and the world) – and you can change your behavior – the things you do. That is all you really have any control over anyway. Unfortunately, most of us are so run by our habits that we never change our behavior. We get stuck in our conditioned responses – to our spouses and our children, to our colleagues at work, to our customers and our clients, to our students, and to the world at large. We are a bundle of conditioned reflexes that operate outside of our control. You have to regain control of your thoughts, your images, your dreams and daydreams, and your behavior. Everything you think, say, and do needs to become intentional and aligned with your purpose, your values, and your goals.

If You Don't Like Your Outcomes, Change Your Responses

Let's look at some examples of how this works.

Do you remember the Northridge earthquake in 1994? Well, I do! I lived through it in Los Angeles. Two days later, I watched as CNN interviewed people commuting to work. The earthquake had damaged one of the main free-ways leading into the city. Traffic was at a standstill, and what was normally a 1-hour drive had become a 2- or 3-hour drive.

The CNN reporter knocked on the window of one of the cars stuck in traffic and asked the driver how he was doing.

He responded angrily, "I hate California. First there were fires, then floods, and now an earthquake! No matter what time I leave in the morning, I'm going to be late for work. I can't believe it!"

**"What do we make where I work?
Mostly we make excuses."**

Then the reporter knocked on the window of the car behind him and asked the second driver the same question. This driver was all smiles. He replied, "It's no problem.

I left my house at five am. I don't think under the circumstances my boss can ask for more than that. I have lots of music cassettes and my Spanish-language tapes with me. I've got my cell phone. I have coffee in a thermos, my lunch – I even brought a book to read. So I'm fine."

Now, if the earthquake or the traffic were really the deciding variables, then everyone should have been angry. But everyone wasn't. It was their individual *response* to the traffic that gave them their particular *outcome*. It was thinking negative thoughts or thinking positive thoughts, leaving the house prepared or leaving the house unprepared that made the difference. It was all a matter of attitude and behavior that created their completely different experiences.

I've Heard There's Going to be a Recession; I've Decided Not to Participate

A friend of mine owns a Lexus dealership in Southern California. When the Gulf War broke out, people stopped coming in to buy Lexuses (or Lexi, for any fellow Harvard graduates and Latin students out there). They knew that if they didn't change their response (R) to the event (E) of nobody coming into the showroom, they were going to slowly go out of business. Their normal response (R) would have been to continue placing ads in the newspaper and on the radio, then wait for people to come in-to the dealership. But that wasn't working. The outcome (O) they were getting was a steady decrease in sales. So they tried a number of new things. The one that worked was driving a fleet of new cars out to where the rich peo-ple were – the country clubs, marinas, polo grounds, par-ties in Beverly Hills and Westlake Village – and then inviting them to take a spin in a new Lexus.

Now think about this … have you ever test-driven a new car and then got back into your old car? Remember that feeling of dissatisfaction you felt as you compared your old car to the new car you had just driven? Your old car was fine up until then. But suddenly you knew there was something better – and you wanted it. The same thing happened with these folks. After test-driving the new car, a high percentage of the people bought or leased a new Lexus.

The dealership had changed their response (R) to an unexpected event (E) – the war – until they got the out-come (O) they wanted … increased sales. They actually ended up selling more cars per week than before the war broke out.

Everything You Experience Today Is the Result of Choices You Have Made in the Past

Everything you experience in life – both internally and externally – is the result of how you have responded to a previous event.

Event: You are given a $400 bonus.
Response: You spend it on a night on the town.
Outcome: You are broke.

Event: You are given a $400 bonus.
Response: You invest it in your mutual fund.
Outcome: You have an increased net worth.

You only have control over three things in your life – the thoughts you think, the images you visualize, and the actions you take (your behavior). How you use these three things determines everything you experience. If you don't like what you are producing and experiencing, you have to change your responses. Change your negative thoughts to positive ones. Change what you daydream about. Change your habits. Change what you read. Change your friends. Change how you talk.

If You Keep on Doing What You've Always Done, You'll Keep on Getting What You've Always Got

Twelve-step programs such as Alcoholics Anonymous define *insanity* as "continuing the same behavior and expecting a different result." It ain't gonna happen! If you are an alcoholic and you keep on drinking, your life is not going to get any better. Likewise, if you continue your current behaviors, your life is not going to get any better either.

The day you change your responses is the day your life will begin to get better! If what you are currently doing would produce the "more" and "better" that you are seeking in life, the more and better would have already shown up! If you want something different, you are going to have to *do* something different!

You Have to Give Up Blaming

All blame is a waste of time. No matter how much fault you find with another, and regardless of how much you blame him, it will not change you.

Wayne Dyer Coauthor of *How to Get What You Really, Really, Really, Really Want*

You will never become successful as long as you continue to blame someone or something else for your lack of success. If you are going to be a winner, you have to acknowledge the truth – it is *you* who took the actions, thought the thoughts, created the feelings, and made the choices that got you to where you now are. It was you!

You are the one who ate the junk food.
You are the one who didn't say no!
You are the one who took the job.
You are the one who stayed in the job.
You are the one who chose to believe them.
You are the one who ignored your intuition.
You are the one who abandoned your dream.
You are the one who bought it.
You are the one who didn't take care of it.
You are the one who decided you had to do it alone.
You are the one who trusted him.
You are the one who said yes to the dogs.

In short, you thought the thoughts, you created the feelings, you made the choice, you said the words, and that's why you are where you are now.

©Tribune Media Services, Inc.
All Rights Reserved

You Have to Give Up Complaining

The man who complains about the way the ball bounces is likely the one who dropped it.

Lou Holtz – The only coach in NCAA history to lead six different college teams to postseason bowl games, and winner of a national championship and "coach of the year" honors

Let's take a moment to really look at complaining. In order

to complain about something or someone, you have to believe that something better exists. You have to have a reference point of something you prefer that you are not willing to take responsibility for creating. Let's look at that more closely.

If you didn't believe there was something better possible – more money, a bigger house, a more fulfilling job, more fun, a more loving spouse – you couldn't complain. So you have this image of something better and you know you would prefer it, but you are unwilling to take the risks that would be required to create it.

Think about this ... people only complain about things they can do something about. We don't complain about the things we have no power over. Have you ever heard anyone complain about gravity? No, never. Have you ever seen an elderly person all bent over with age walking down the street complaining about gravity? Of course not.

But why not? If it weren't for gravity, people wouldn't fall down the stairs, planes wouldn't fall out of the sky, and we wouldn't break any dishes. But nobody complains about it. And the reason is because gravity just exists. There is nothing anyone can do about gravity, so we just accept it. We know that complaining will not change it, so we don't complain about it. In fact, because it just is, we use gravity to our advantage. We build aqueducts down mountainsides to carry water to us, and we use drains to take away our waste.

Even more interesting is that we choose to play with gravity, to have fun with it. Almost every sport we play uses gravity. We ski, sky-dive, high-jump, throw the discus and the javelin, and play basketball, baseball, and golf – all of which require gravity.

The circumstances you complain about are, by their very nature, situations you can change – but you have chosen not to. You can get a better job, find a more loving partner, make more money, live in a nicer house, live in a better neighborhood, and eat healthier food. But all of these things would require you to change.

If you refer to the list found earlier in this chapter, you could

Learn to cook healthier food.
Say no in the face of peer pressure.
Quit and find a better job.
Take the time to conduct due diligence.
Trust your own gut feelings.
Go back to school to pursue your dream.
Take better care of your possessions.
Reach out for help.
Ask others to assist you.
Take a self-development class.
Sell or give away the dogs.

But why don't you simply do those things? It's because they involve risks. You run the risk of being unemployed, left alone, or ridiculed and judged by others. You run the risk of failure, confrontation, or being wrong. You run the risk of your mother, your neighbors, or your spouse disapproving of you. Making a change might take effort, money, and time. It might be uncomfortable, difficult, or confusing. And so, to avoid risking any of those uncomfortable feelings and experiences, you stay put and complain about it.

As I stated before, complaining means you have a reference point for something better that you would prefer but that you are unwilling to take the risk of creating. Either accept that you are making the choice to stay where you are, take responsibility for your choice, and stop complaining ... or ... take the risk of creating your life exactly the way you want it.

If you want to get from where you are to where you want to be, of course you're going to have to take that risk.

So make the decision to stop complaining, to stop spending time with complainers, and get on with creating the life of your dreams.

You're Complaining to the Wrong Person

Have you ever noticed that people almost always complain to the wrong people – to people who can't do anything about their complaint? They go to work and complain about their spouse; then they come home and complain to their spouse about the people at work. Why? Because it's easier; it's less risky. It takes courage to tell your spouse that you are not happy with the way things are at home. It takes courage to ask for a behavioral change. It also takes courage to ask your boss to plan better so that you don't end up working every weekend. But only your boss can do anything about that. Your spouse can't.

Learn to replace complaining with making requests and taking action that will achieve your desired outcomes. That is what successful people do. That is what works. If you find yourself in a situation you don't like, either work to make it better or leave. Do something to change it or get the heck out. Agree to work on the relationship or get a divorce. Work to improve working conditions or find a new job. Either way, you will get a change. As the old adage says, "Don't just sit there (and complain), do something." And remember, it's up to you to make the change, to do something different. The world doesn't owe you anything. You have to create it.

You Either Create or Allow Everything That Happens to You

To be powerful, you need to take the position that you create or allow everything that happens to you. By *create*, I mean that you directly cause something to happen by your actions or inactions. If you walk up to a man in a bar who is bigger than you, has obviously been drinking for a long time, and say to him, "You are really ugly and stupid," and he jumps off the bar stool, hits you in the jaw, and you end up in the hospital – you created that. That's an easy-to-understand example.

Here's one that may be harder to swallow: You work late every night. You come home tired and burned out. You eat dinner in a coma and then sit down in front of the television to watch a basketball game. You're too tired and stressed out to do anything else – like go for a walk or play with the kids. This goes on for years. Your wife asks you to talk to her. You say, "Later!" Three years later, you come home to an empty house and a note that she has left you and taken the kids. You created that one, too!

Other times, we simply allow things to happen to us by our inaction and our unwillingness to do what is necessary to create or maintain what we want:

- You didn't follow through on your threat to take away privileges if the kids didn't clean up after themselves, and now the house looks like a war zone.
- You didn't demand he join you in counseling or leave the first time he hit you, so now you're still getting hit.
- You didn't attend any sales and motivational seminars because you were too busy, and now the new kid just won the top sales award.
- You didn't take the time to take the dogs to obedience training, and now they're out of control.
- You didn't take time to maintain your car, and now you're sitting by the side of the road with your car broken down.

- You didn't go back to school, and now you are being passed over for a promotion.

Realize that you are not the victim here. You stood passively by and let it happen. You didn't say anything, make a demand, make a request, say no, try something new, or leave.

Yellow Alerts

Be aware that nothing ever just "happens" to you. Just like the "yellow alerts" in the old *Star Trek* television series, you almost always receive advance warnings – in the form of telltale signs, comments from others, gut instinct, or intuition – that alert you to the impending danger and give you time to prevent the unwanted outcome.

You are getting yellow alerts all the time. There are *external* yellow alerts:

He keeps coming home later and later with alcohol on his breath
The client's first check bounced
He screamed at his secretary
His mother warned you
Your friends told you

And there are *internal* yellow alerts:

That feeling in your stomach

That inkling you had
That fleeting thought that just maybe …
That intuition
That fear that emerged
That dream that woke you up in the middle of
   the night

We have a whole language that informs us:

Clues, inklings, suspicions
The handwriting on the wall
I had a feeling that …
I could see it coming for a mile
My gut feeling told me

These alerts give you time to change your response (R) in the E + R = O equation. However, too many people ignore the yellow alerts because paying attention to them would require them to do something that is uncomfortable. It is uncomfortable to confront your spouse about the cigarettes in the ashtray that have lipstick on them. It is uncomfortable to speak up in a staff meeting when you are the only one who feels that the proposed plan won't work. It is uncomfortable to tell someone you don't trust them.

So you pretend not to see and not to know because it is easier, more convenient and less uncomfortable, avoids confrontation, keeps the peace, and protects you from having to take risks.

Life Becomes Much Easier

Successful people, on the other hand, face facts squarely. They do the uncomfortable and take steps to create their desired outcomes. Successful people don't wait for disasters to occur and then blame something or someone else for their problems.

Once you begin to respond quickly and decisively to signals and events as they occur, life becomes much easier. You start seeing improved outcomes both internally and externally. Old internal self-talk such as "I feel like a victim; I feel used; nothing ever seems to work out for me" is replaced with "I feel great; I am in control; I can make things happen."

External outcomes such as "Nobody ever comes to our store; we missed our quarterly goals; people are complaining that our new product doesn't work" are transformed into "We have more money in the bank; I lead the division in sales; our product is flying off the shelves."

It's Simple

The bottom line is that you are the one who is creating your life the way it is. The life you currently live is the result of all of your past thoughts and actions. You are in charge of your current thoughts and your present feelings. You are in charge of what you say and what you do. You are also in charge of what goes into your mind – the books and magazines you read, the movies and television shows you watch, and the people you hang out with. Every action is under your control. To be more successful, all you have to do is act in ways that produce more of what you want.

That's it. It's that simple!

Simple Isn't Necessarily Easy

Though this principle is simple, it is not necessarily easy to implement. It requires concentrated awareness, dedicated discipline, and a willingness to experiment and take risks. You have to be willing to pay attention to what you are doing and to the results you are producing. You have to ask yourself, your family, your friends, your colleagues, your managers, your teachers, your coaches, and your clients for feedback. "Is what I'm doing working? Could I be doing it better? Is there something more I should be doing that I am not? Is there something I am doing that I should stop doing? How do you see me limiting myself?"

Don't be afraid to ask. Most people are afraid to ask for feedback about how they are doing because they are afraid of what they are going to hear. There is nothing to be afraid of. The truth is the truth. You are better off knowing the truth than not knowing it. And once you know, you can do something about it. You cannot improve your life, your relationships, your game, or your performance without feedback.

Slow down and pay attention. Life will always give you feedback about the effects of your behavior if you will just pay attention. If your golf ball is always slicing to the right, if you're not making sales, if you're getting C's in all your college courses, if your children are mad at you, if your body is tired and weak, if your house is a mess, or if you're not happy – this is all feedback. It is telling you that something is wrong. This is the time to start paying attention to what is happening.

Ask yourself: *How am I creating or allowing this to happen? What am I doing that's working that I need to be doing more of? (Should I do more practicing, meditating, delegating, trusting, listening, asking questions, keeping my eye on the ball, advertising, saying "I love you," controlling my carbohydrate intake?)*

What am I doing that's not working? What do I need to be doing less of? (Am I talking too much, watching too much television, spending too much money, eating too much sugar, drinking too much, being late too often, gossiping, putting other people down?)

What am I not doing that I need to try on to see if it works? (Do I need to listen more, exercise, get more sleep, drink more water, ask for help, do more marketing, read, plan, communicate, delegate, follow through, hire a coach, volunteer, or be more appreciative?)

This book is full of proven success principles and techniques you can immediately put into practice in your life. You will have to suspend judgment, take a leap of faith, act as if they are true, and try them out. Only then will you have firsthand experience about their effectiveness for your life. You won't know if they work unless you give them a try. And here's the rub – no one else can do this for you. Only you can do it.

But the formula is simple – do more of what is working, do less of what isn't, and try on new behaviors to see if they produce better results.

Pay Attention …
Your Results Don't Lie

The easiest, fastest, and best way to find out what is or isn't working is to pay attention to the results you are currently producing. You are either rich or you are not. You either command respect or you don't. You are either golfing par or you are not. You are either maintaining your ideal body weight or you are not. You are either happy or you are not. You either have what you want or you don't. It's that simple. Results don't lie!

You have to give up the excuses and justifications and come to terms with the results you are producing. If you are under quota or overweight, all the great reasons in the world won't change that. The only thing that will change your results is to change your behavior. Prospect more, get some sales training, change your sales presentation, change your diet, consume fewer calories, and exercise more frequently – these are things that will make a difference. But you have to first be willing to look at the results you are producing. The only starting point that works is reality.

So start paying attention to what is so. Look around at your life and the people in it. Are you and they happy? Is there balance, beauty, comfort, and ease? Do your systems work? Are you getting what you want? Is your net worth increasing? Are your grades satisfactory? Are you healthy, fit, and pain free? Are you getting better in all areas of your life? If not, then something needs to happen, and only you can make it happen.

Don't kid yourself. Be ruthlessly honest with yourself. Take your own inventory.

Be Clear Why You're Here

Learn to get in touch with the silence within yourself
and know that everything in life has a purpose.

Elisabeth Kubler-Ross, M.D. – Psychiatrist
and author of the classic *On Death and Dying*

I believe each of us is born with a life purpose. Identifying, acknowledging, and honoring this purpose is perhaps the most important action successful people take. They take the time to understand what they're here to do – and then they pursue that with passion and enthusiasm.

What Were You Put on This Earth to Do?

I discovered long ago what I was put on this earth to do. I determined my true purpose in life, my "right livelihood." I discovered how to inject passion and determination into every activity I undertake. And I learned how purpose can bring an aspect of fun and fulfillment to virtually everything I do.

Now I'd like to help uncover the same secret for you.

You see, without a purpose in life, it's easy to get sidetracked on your life's journey. It's easy to wander and drift, accomplishing little.

But with a purpose, everything in life seems to fall into place. To be "on purpose" means you're doing what you love to do, doing what you're good at and accomplishing what's important to you. When you truly are on purpose, the people, resources, and opportunities you need naturally gravitate toward you. The world benefits, too, because when you act in alignment with your true life purpose, all of your actions automatically serve others.

Some Personal Life Purpose Statements

My life purpose is *to inspire and empower people to live their highest vision in a context of love and joy*. I inspire people to live their highest vision (see Principle 3, "Decide What You Want") by collecting and disseminating inspiring stories through the *Chicken Soup for the Soul*® series and in my inspirational keynote speeches. I empower people to live their dreams by writing practical self-help books like this one, *The Power of Focus*, and *The Aladdin Factor*; designing courses for high school students; and conducting seminars and workshops for adults that teach powerful tools for creating one's ideal life.

Here are the life purpose statements of some of my friends. It is important to note that they have all become self-made millionaires through the fulfillment of their life purpose.

- To inspire and empower people to achieve their destiny[1]
- To uplift humanity's consciousness through business[2]
- To humbly serve the Lord by being a loving, playful, powerful, and passionate example of the absolute joy that is available to us the moment we rejoice in God's gifts and sincerely love and serve all of his creations[3]
- To leave the world a better place than I found it, for horses and for people, too[4]
- To create and inspire one million millionaires who each give $1 million to their church or charity[5]
- To educate and inspire people to live their highest self based in courage, purpose, and joy, versus fear, need, and obligation[6]

Decide upon your major definite purpose in life and then organize all your activities around it.

Brian Tracy – One of America's leading authorities on the development of human potential and personal effectiveness

Once you know what your life purpose is, you can organize all of your activities around it. Everything you do should be an expression of your purpose. If an activity doesn't fit that formula, you wouldn't work on it. Period.

What's the "Why" Behind Everything You Do?

Without purpose as the compass to guide you, your goals and action plans may not ultimately fulfill you. You don't want to get to the top of the ladder only to find out you had it leaning up against the wrong wall.

When Julie Laipply was a child, she was a very big fan of animals. As a result, all she ever heard growing up was "Julie, you should be a vet. You're going to be a great vet. That's what you should do." So when she got to Ohio State University, she took biology, anatomy, and chemistry, and started studying to be a vet. A Rotary Ambassadorial Scholarship allowed her to spend her senior year studying in Manchester, England. Away from the family and faculty pressures back home, she found herself one dreary day sitting at her desk, surrounded by biology books and staring out the window, when it suddenly hit her: *You know what? I'm totally miserable. Why am I so miserable? What am I doing? I don't want to be a vet!*

Julie then asked herself, *What is a job I would love so much that I'd do it for free but that I could actually get paid for? It's not being a vet. That's not the right job.* Then she thought back over all the things she'd done in her life and what had made her the most happy. And then it hit her – it was all of the youth leadership conferences that she had volunteered at, and the communications and leadership courses she had taken as elective courses back at Ohio

State. *How could I have been so ignorant? Here I am at my fourth year at school and just finally realizing I'm on the wrong path and not doing the right thing. But it's been here in front of me the whole time. I just never took the time to acknowledge it until now.*

Buoyed by her new insight, Julie spent the rest of her year in England taking courses in communications and media performance. When she returned to Ohio State, she was eventually able to convince the administration to let her create her own program in "leadership studies," and while it took her 2 years longer to finally graduate, she went on to become a senior management consultant in leadership training and development for the Pentagon. She also won the Miss Virginia USA contest, which allowed her to spend much of 2002 speaking to kids all across Virginia, and more recently she has created the Role Models and Mentors for Youth Foundation, which teaches kids how to be better role models for one another. By the way, Julie is only 26 years old – a testament to the power that clarity of purpose can create in your life.

The good news is that you don't have to spend a year abroad to get away from the daily pressures of your life long enough to create the space to discover what you are really here to do. You can simply take the time to complete two simple exercises that will help you clarify your purpose.

Your Inner Guidance System Is Your Joy

It is the soul's duty to be loyal to its own desires.
It must abandon itself to its master passion.

Dame Rebecca West – Best-selling author

You were born with an inner guidance system that tells you when you are on or off purpose by the amount of joy you are experiencing. The things that bring you the greatest joy are in alignment with your purpose. To begin to home in on your purpose, make a list of the times you have felt most joyful and alive. What are the common elements of these experiences? Can you figure out a way to make a living doing these things?

Pat Williams is the senior vice-president of the Orlando Magic basketball team. He has also written 36 books and is a professional speaker. When I asked him what he felt the greatest secret to success was, he replied, "Figure out what you love to do as young as you can, and then organize your life around figuring out how to make a living at it." For young Pat, it was sports – more specifically, baseball. When his father took him to his first baseball game in Philadelphia, he fell in love with the game. He learned to read by reading the sports section of the *New York Times*. He knew he wanted to grow up and have a career in sports. He devoted almost every waking moment to it. He collected baseball cards, played sports, and wrote a sports column for the school newspaper.

Pat went on to have a career in the front office of the Philadelphia Phillies baseball team, then with the Philadelphia 76ers basketball team. When the NBA considered granting an expansion team franchise to Orlando, Pat was there to lead the fight. Now in his sixties, Pat has enjoyed 40-plus years doing what he loves, and he has enjoyed every minute of it. Once you are clear about what brings you the greatest joy, you will have a major insight into your purpose.

This second exercise is a simple but powerful way to create a compelling statement of your life purpose to guide and direct your behavior. Take time now to complete the following exercise.

The Life Purpose Exercise[7]

1. List two of your unique personal qualities, such as *enthusiasm* and *creativity*.

   ....

2. List one or two ways you enjoy expressing those qualities when interacting with others, such as *to support* and *to inspire*.

   ....

3. Assume the world is perfect right now. What does this world look like? How is everyone interacting with everyone else? What does it feel like? Write your answer as a statement, in the present tense, describing the ultimate condition, the perfect world as you see it and feel it. Remember, a perfect world is a fun place to be.

   EXAMPLE: Everyone is freely expressing their own unique talents. Everyone is working in harmony. Everyone is expressing love.

4. Combine the three prior subdivisions of this paragraph into a single statement.

   EXAMPLE: My purpose is to use my creativity and enthusiasm to support and inspire others to freely express their talents in a harmonious and loving way.

Staying on Purpose

Once you have determined and written down your life purpose, read it every day, preferably in the morning. If you are artistic or strongly visual by nature, you may want to draw or paint a symbol or picture that represents your life purpose and then hang it somewhere (on the refrigerator, opposite your desk, near your bed) where you will see it every day. This will keep you focused on your purpose.

As you read on over the next few Principles and define your vision and your goals, make sure they are aligned with and serve to fulfill your purpose.

Another approach to clarifying your purpose is to set aside some time for quiet reflection – time for a period of meditation. After you become relaxed and enter into a state of deep self-love and peacefulness, ask yourself, *What is my purpose for living?* or *What is my unique role in the universe?* Allow the answer to simply come to you. Let it be as expansive as you can imagine. The words that come need not be flowery or poetic; what is important is how inspired the words make you feel.

Principle 3

Decide What You Want

The indispensable first step to getting the things you
want out of life is this: decide what you want.

Ben Stein – Actor and author

Once you have decided why you are here, you have to decide what you want to do, be, and have. What do you
want to accomplish? What do you want to experience?
And what possessions do you want to acquire? In the journey from where you are to where you want to be, you
have to decide where you want to be. In other words,
what does success look like to you?

One of the main reasons why most people don't get
what they want is they haven't decided what they want.
They haven't defined their desires in clear and compelling
detail.

Early Childhood Programming Often Gets in the Way of What You Want

Inside of every one of us is that tiny seed of the "you" that you were meant to become. Unfortunately, you may have buried this seed in response to your parents, teachers, coaches, and other adult role models as you were growing up.

You started out as a baby knowing exactly what you wanted. You knew when you were hungry. You spit out the foods you didn't like and avidly devoured the ones you did. You had no trouble expressing your needs and wants. You simply cried loudly – with no inhibitions or holding back – until you got what you wanted. You had everything inside of you that you needed to get fed, changed, held, and rocked. As you got older, you crawled around and moved toward whatever held the most interest for you. You were clear about what you wanted, and you headed straight toward it with no fear.

So what happened?

Somewhere along the way, someone said …

Don't touch that!
Stay away from there.
Keep your hands off that.
Eat everything on your plate whether you like it or not!
You don't really feel that way.

You don't really want that.
You should be ashamed of yourself.
Stop crying. Don't be such a baby.

As you got older, you heard …

You can't have everything you want simply because
you want it.
Money doesn't grow on trees.
Can't you think of anybody but yourself?!
Stop being so selfish!
Stop doing what you are doing and come do what I
want you to do!

Don't Live Someone Else's Dreams

After many years of these kinds of sanctions, most of us
eventually lost touch with the needs of our bodies and
the desires of our hearts and somehow got stuck trying to
figure out what other people wanted us to do. We learned
how to act and how to be to get *their* approval. As a result,
we now do a lot of things we don't want to do but that
please a lot of other people:

• We go to medical school because that is what Dad
wanted for us.

- We get married to please our mother.
- We get a "real job" instead of pursuing our dream career in the arts.
- We go straight into graduate school instead of taking a year off and backpacking through Europe.

In the name of being sensible, we end up becoming numb to our own desires. It's no wonder that when we ask many teenagers what they want to do or be, they honestly answer, "I don't know." There are too many layers of "should's," "ought to's," and "you'd better's" piled on top of and suffocating what they really want.

So how do you reclaim yourself and your true desires? How do you get back to what you really want with no fear, shame, or inhibition? How do you reconnect with your real passion?

You start on the smallest level by honoring your preferences in every situation – no matter how large or small. Don't think of them as petty. They might be inconsequential to someone else, but they are not to you.

Stop Settling for Less Than You Want

If you are going to reown your power and get what you really want out of life, you will have to stop saying, "I don't know; I don't care; it doesn't matter to me" – or the current

favorite of teenagers, "Whatever." When you are confront-
ed with a choice, no matter how small or insignificant, act
as if you have a preference. Ask yourself, *If I did know,
what would it be? If I did care, which would I prefer? If it did
matter, what would I rather do?*

Not being clear about what you want and making other people's needs and desires more important than your
own is simply a habit. You can break it by practicing the
opposite habit.

The Yellow Notebook

Many years ago, I took a workshop with self-esteem and
motivational expert Chérie Carter-Scott, author of *If Life Is
a Game, These Are the Rules*. As the 24 of us entered the
training room on the first morning, we were directed to
take a seat in one of the chairs facing the front of the room.
There was a spiral-bound notebook on every chair. Some
were blue, some were yellow, some were red. The one on
my chair was yellow. I remember thinking, *I hate yellow.
I wish I had a blue one.*

Then Chérie said something that changed my life forever:
"If you don't like the color of the notebook you have, trade
with someone else and get the one you want. You deserve to
have everything in your life exactly the way you want it."

Wow, what a radical concept! For 20-some years, I had
not operated from that premise. I had settled, thinking I
couldn't have everything I wanted.

So I turned to the person to my right and said, "Would you mind trading your blue notebook for my yellow one?"

She responded, "Not at all. I prefer yellow. I like the brightness of the color. It fits my mood." I now had my blue notebook. Not a huge success in the greater scheme of things, but it was the beginning of reclaiming my birthright to acknowledge my preferences and get exactly what I want. Up until then, I would have discounted my preference as petty and not worth acting on. I would have continued to numb out my awareness of what I wanted. That day was a turning point for me – the beginning of allowing myself to know and act on my wants and desires in a much more powerful way.

Make an "I Want" List

One of the easiest ways to begin clarifying what you truly want is to make a list of 30 things you want to do, 30 things you want to have, and 30 things you want to be before you die. This is a great way to get the ball rolling.

Another powerful technique to unearth your wants is to ask a friend to help you make an "I Want" list. Have your friend continually ask, "What do you want? What do you want?" for 10 to 15 minutes, and jot down your answers. You'll find the first wants aren't all that profound. In fact, most people usually hear themselves saying, "I want a Mercedes. I want a big house on the ocean." And so on.

However, by the end of the 15-minute exercise, the real you begins to speak: "I want people to love me. I want to express myself. I want to make a difference. I want to feel powerful" … wants that are true expressions of your core values.

Is Worrying About Making a Living Stopping You?

What often stops people from expressing their true desire is they don't think they can make a living doing what they love to do.

"What I love to do is hang out and talk with people," you might say.

Well, Oprah Winfrey makes a living hanging out talking with people. And my friend Diane Brause, who is an international tour guide, makes a living hanging out talking with people in some of the most exciting and exotic locations in the world.

Tiger Woods loves to play golf. Ellen DeGeneres loves to make people laugh. My sister loves to design jewelry and hang out with teenagers. Donald Trump loves to make deals and build buildings. I love to read and share what I have learned with others in books, speeches, and workshops. It's possible to make a living doing what you love.

Make a list of 20 things you love to do, and then think

of ways you can make a living doing some of those things. If you love sports, you could play sports, be a sportswriter or photographer, or work in sports management as an agent or in the front office of a professional team. You could be a coach, a manager, or a scout. You could be a broadcaster, a camera operator, or a team publicist. There are myriad ways to make money in any field that you love.

For now just decide what you would like to do, and in the following chapters I'll show you how to be successful and make money at it.

Clarify Your Vision of Your Ideal Life

To get from where you are to where you want to be, you have to know two things – where you are and where you want to get to. Your vision is a detailed description of where you want to get to. It describes in detail what your destination looks like and feels like. To create a balanced and successful life, your vision needs to include the following seven areas: work and career, finances, recreation and free time, health and fitness, relationships, personal goals, and contribution to the larger community.

At this stage in the journey, it is not necessary to know exactly how you are going to get there. All that is important is that you figure out where there is. If you get clear on the what, the how will be taken care of.

Your Inner Global Positioning System

The process of getting from where you are to where you want to be is like using the navigational system with GPS (Global Positioning System) technology in a newer-model car. For the system to work, it simply needs to know where you are and where you want to go. The navigation system figures out where you are by the use of an onboard computer that receives signals from three satellites and calculates your exact position. When you type in your destination, the navigational system plots a perfect course for you. All you have to do is follow the instructions.

Success in life works the same way. All you have to do is decide where you want to go by clarifying your vision, lock in the destination through goal-setting, affirmations, and visualization, and start moving in the right direction. Your inner GPS will keep unfolding your route as you continue to move forward. In other words, once you clarify and stay focused on your vision, the exact steps will keep appearing along the way. Once you are clear about what you want and keep your mind constantly focused on it, the how will keep showing up – sometimes just when you need it and not a moment earlier.

High Achievers
Have Bigger Visions

> The greater danger for most of us is not that our aim
> is too high and we miss it, but that it is too low and
> we reach it.
>
> Michelangelo

I want to encourage you not to limit your vision in any
way. Let it be as big as it is. When I interviewed Dave Liniger, the CEO of RE/MAX, the USA's largest real estate company, he told me, "Always dream big dreams. Big dreams
attract big people." General Wesley Clark recently told me,
"It doesn't take any more energy to create a big dream than
it does to create a little one." My experience is that one of
the few differences between the superachievers and the
rest of the world is that the superachievers simply dream
bigger. John F. Kennedy dreamed of putting a man on the
moon. Martin Luther King Jr. dreamed of a country free of
prejudice and injustice. Bill Gates dreams of a world in
which every home has a computer that is connected to the
Internet. Buckminster Fuller dreamed of a world where
everybody had access to electrical power.

These high achievers see the world from a whole different perspective – as a place where amazing things can happen, where billions of lives can be improved, where new
technology can change the way we live, and where the
world's resources can be leveraged for the greatest possible

© 2001 Randay Glasbergen. www.glasbergen.com

**"I'm wealthy beyond my wildest dreams!
Unfortunately, my dreams were never very wild."**

mutual gain. They believe anything is possible, and they believe they have an integral part in creating it.

When Mark Victor Hansen and I first published *Chicken Soup for the Soul*®, what we call our "2020 vision" was also a big one – to sell 1 billion *Chicken Soup* books and to raise $500 million for charity through tithing a portion of all of our profits by the year 2020. We were and are very clear about what we want to accomplish.

If you limit your choices only to what seems possible or reasonable, you disconnect yourself from what you truly want, and all that is left is a compromise.

Robert Fritz – Author of *The Path of Least Resistance*

Don't Let Anyone Talk You Out of Your Vision

There are people who will try to talk you out of your vision. They will tell you that you are crazy and that it can't be done. There will be those who will laugh at you and try to bring you down to their level. My friend Monty Roberts, the author of *The Man Who Listens to Horses*, calls these people dream-stealers. Don't listen to them.

When Monty was in high school, his teacher gave the class the assignment to write about what they wanted to do when they grew up. Monty wrote that he wanted to own his own 200-acre ranch and raise Thoroughbred racehorses. His teacher gave him an F and explained that the grade reflected that he deemed his dream unrealistic. No boy who was living in a camper on the back of a pick-up truck would ever be able to amass enough money to buy a ranch, purchase breeding stock, and pay the necessary salaries for ranch hands. When he offered Monty the chance of rewriting his paper for a higher grade, Monty told him, "You keep the F; I'm keeping my dream."

Today Monty's 154-acre Flag Is Up Farms in Solvang, California, raises Thoroughbred racehorses and trains hundreds of horse trainers in a more humane way to "join up" with and train horses.[1]

The Vision Exercise

Create your future from your future, not your past.

Werner Erhard – Founder of EST training and the Landmark Forum

The following exercise is designed to help you clarify your vision. Although you could do this as a strictly mental exercise by just thinking about the answers and then writing them down, I want to encourage you to go deeper than that. If you do, you'll get deeper answers that serve you better.

Start by putting on some relaxing music and sitting quietly in a comfortable environment where you won't be disturbed. Then, close your eyes and ask your subconscious mind to give you images of what your ideal life would look like if you could have it exactly the way you want it, in each of the following categories:

1. First, focus on the financial area of your life. What is your annual income? What does your cash flow look like? How much money do you have in savings and investments? What is your total net worth?

   Next ... what does your home look like? Where is it located? Does it have a view? What kind of yard and landscaping does it have? Is there a pool or a stable for horses? What color are the walls? What does the furniture look like? Are there paintings hanging in the rooms? What do they look like? Walk through your perfect house, filling in all of the details.

At this point, don't worry about how you'll get that house. Don't sabotage yourself by saying, "I can't live in Malibu because I don't make enough money." Once you give your mind's eye the picture, your mind will solve the "not enough money" challenge.

Next, visualize what kind of car you are driving and any other important possessions your finances have provided.

2. Next, visualize your ideal job or career. Where are you working? What are you doing? With whom are you working? What kind of clients or customers do you have? What is your compensation like? Is it your own business?

3. Then, focus on your free time, your recreation time. What are you doing with your family and friends in the free time you've created for yourself? What hobbies are you pursuing? What kinds of vacations do you take? What do you do for fun?

4. Next, what is your ideal vision of your body and your physical health? Are you free of all disease? How long do you live to? Are you open, relaxed, in an ecstatic state of bliss all day long? Are you full of vitality? Are you flexible as well as strong? Do you exercise, eat good food, and drink lots of water?

5. Then move on to your ideal vision of your relationships with your family and friends. What is your relationship with your family like? Who are your friends? What is the quality of your relationships with your friends? What do those friendships feel like? Are they loving, supportive, empowering? What kinds of things do you do together?

6. What about the personal arena of your life? Do you see yourself going back to school, getting training, attending workshops, seeking therapy for a past hurt, or growing spiritually? Do you meditate or go on spiritual retreats with your church? Do you want to learn to play an instrument or write your autobiography? Do you want to run a marathon or take an art class? Do you want to travel to other countries?

7. Finally, focus on the community you live in, the community you've chosen. What does it look like when it is operating perfectly? What kinds of community activities take place there? What about your charitable work? What do you do to help others and make a difference? How often do you participate in these activities? Who are you helping?

You can write down your answers as you go, or you can do the whole exercise first and then open your eyes and write them down. In either case, make sure you capture everything in writing as soon as you complete the exercise.

Every day, review the vision you have written down. This will keep your conscious and subconscious minds focused on your vision, and as you apply the other principles and tools in the book, you will begin to manifest all the different aspects of your vision.

Share Your Vision
for Maximum Impact

When you've finished writing down your vision, share your vision with a good friend whom you can trust to be positive and supportive. You might be afraid that your friend will think your vision is too outlandish, impossible to achieve, too idealistic, unrealistic, or materialistic. Almost all people have these thoughts when they think about sharing their vision. But the truth is, most people, deep down in their hearts, want the very same things you want. Everyone wants financial abundance, a comfortable home, meaningful work they enjoy, good health, time to do the things they love, nurturing relationships with their family and friends, and an opportunity to make a difference in the world. But too few of us readily admit it.

You'll find that when you share your vision, some people will want to help you make it happen. Others will introduce you to friends and resources that can help you. You'll also find that each time that you share your vision, it becomes clearer and feels more real and attainable. And most importantly, every time you share your vision, you strengthen your own subconscious belief that you can achieve it.

Principle 4

Believe It's Possible

The number one problem that keeps people
from winning in the United States today is
lack of belief in themselves.

Arthur L. Williams – Founder of A.L. Williams Insurance Company,
which was sold to Primerica for $90 million in 1989

Napoleon Hill once said, "Whatever the mind can conceive and believe, it can achieve." In fact, the mind is such a powerful instrument, it can deliver to you literally everything you want. But you have to *believe* that what you want is possible.

You Get What You Expect

Scientists used to believe that humans responded to information flowing into the brain from the outside world. But today, they're learning instead that we respond to what the brain, on the basis of previous experience, expects to happen next.

Doctors in Texas, for example – studying the effect of arthroscopic knee surgery – assigned patients with sore, worn-out knees to one of three surgical procedures:

scraping out the knee joint, washing out the joint, or doing nothing.

During the "nothing" operation, doctors anesthetized the patient, made three incisions in the knee as if to insert their surgical instruments, and then pretended to operate. Two years after surgery, patients who underwent the pretend surgery reported the same amount of relief from pain and swelling as those who had received the actual treatments. The brain *expected* the "surgery" to improve the knee, and it did.

Why does the brain work this way? Neuropsychologists who study expectancy theory say it's because we spend our whole lives becoming conditioned. Through a lifetime's worth of events, our brain actually learns what to expect next – whether it eventually happens that way or not. And because our brain expects something will happen a certain way, we often achieve exactly what we anticipate.

This is why it's so important to hold positive expectations in your mind. When you replace your old negative expectations with more positive ones – when you begin to believe that what you want is possible – your brain will actually take over the job of accomplishing that possibility for you. Better than that, your brain will actually expect to achieve that outcome.[1]

"You Gotta Believe"

> You can be anything you want to be, if only you
> believe with sufficient conviction and act in
> accordance with your faith; for whatever the mind
> can conceive and believe, the mind can achieve.
>
> **Napoleon Hill** – Best-selling author of *Think and Grow Rich*

When Philadelphia Phillies pitcher Tug McGraw – father
of legendary country singer Tim McGraw – struck out batter Willie Wilson to earn the Phillies the 1980 World Series
title, *Sports Illustrated* captured an immortal image of ela-
tion on the pitcher's mound – an image few people knew
was played out *exactly as McGraw had planned it*.

When I had the opportunity to meet Tug one afternoon
in New York, I asked him about his experience on the
mound that day.

"It was as if I'd been there a thousand times before," he
said. "When I was growing up, I would pitch to my father
in the backyard. We would always get to where it was the
bottom of the ninth in the World Series with two outs and
three men on base. I would always bear down and strike
them out." Because Tug had conditioned his brain day after day in the backyard, the day eventually arrived where
he was living that dream for real.

McGraw's reputation as a positive thinker had begun [7]
years earlier during the New York Mets' 1973 National
League championship season, when Tug coined the

phrase "You gotta believe" during one of the team's meetings. That Mets team, in last place in the division in August, went on to win the National League pennant and reach game 7 of the World Series, where they finally succumbed to the Oakland A's.

Another example of his always optimistic "you gotta believe" attitude was the time, while he was a spokesman for the Little League, that he said, "Kids should practice autographing baseballs. This is a skill that's often overlooked in Little League." And then he smiled his infectious smile.

Believe in Yourself and Go for It

Sooner or later, those who win
are those who think they can.

Richard Bach – Best-selling author of *Jonathan Livingston Seagull*

Tim Ferriss believed in himself. In fact, he believed so strongly in his abilities that he won the national San Shou kickboxing title just 6 weeks after being introduced to the sport.

As a prior all-American and judo team captain at Princeton, Tim had always dreamed of winning a national title. He had worked hard. He was good at his sport. But repeated injuries over multiple seasons had continually denied him his dream.

So when a friend called one day to invite Tim to watch

him in the national Chinese kickboxing championships 6 weeks away, Tim instantly decided to join him at the competition.

Because he had never been in any kind of striking competition before, he called USA Boxing and asked where the best trainers could be found. He traveled to a tough neighborhood in Trenton, New Jersey, to learn from boxing coaches who had trained gold medalists. And after 4 grueling hours a day in the ring, he put in more time conditioning in the weight room. To make up for his lack of time in the sport, Tim's trainers focused on exploiting his strengths instead of making up for his weaknesses.

Tim didn't want to merely compete. He wanted to win.

When the competition day at last arrived, Tim defeated three highly acclaimed opponents before making it to the finals. As he anticipated what he would have to do to win in the final match, he closed his eyes and visualized defeating his opponent in the very first round.

Later, Tim told me that most people fail not because they lack the skills or aptitude to reach their goal but because they simply don't believe they can reach it. Tim believed. And won.

It Helps to Have Someone Else Believe in You First

When 20-year-old Ruben Gonzalez showed up at the U.S. Olympic Training Center in Lake Placid, New York, he had in his pocket the business card of a Houston businessman who believed in his Olympic dream. Ruben was there to learn the sport of luge, a sport that 9 of 10 aspirants give up after the first season. Almost everyone breaks more than one bone before mastering this 90-mile-per-hour race against time in an enclosed mile-long downhill track of concrete and ice. But Ruben had a dream, passion, a commitment not to quit, and the support of his friend, Craig, back in Houston.

When Ruben got back to his room after the first day of training, he called up Craig.

"Craig this is nuts! My side hurts. I think I broke my foot. That's it. I am going back to soccer!"

Craig interrupted him. "Ruben, get in front of a mirror!"

"What?"

"I said, 'Get in front of a mirror!' "

Ruben got up, stretched the phone cord, and stood in front of a full-length mirror.

"Now repeat after me: No matter how bad it is, and how bad it gets, I'm going to make it!"

Ruben felt like an idiot staring at himself in the mirror, so in the most wimpy, wishy-washy way possible, he said, "No matter how bad it is, and how bad it gets, I'm going to make it!"

"C'mon! Say it right. You're Mr. Olympic Man! That's all you ever talk about! Are you going to do it or not?"

Ruben started getting serious. "No matter how bad it is, and how bad it gets, I'm going to make it!"

"Again!"

"No matter how bad it is, and how bad it gets, I'm going to make it!"

And again and again and again.

About the fifth time Ruben said it, he thought, *Hey, this feels kind of good. I'm standing a little bit straighter*. By the tenth time he said it, he jumped up in the air and shouted, "I don't care what happens. I'm going to make it. I can break both legs. Bones heal. I'll come back and I will make it. I *will* be an Olympian!"

It's amazing what happens to your self-confidence when you get eyeball to eyeball with yourself and you forcefully tell yourself what you're going to do. Whatever your dream is, look at yourself in the mirror and declare that you are indeed going to achieve it – no matter what the price.

Ruben Gonzalez made that declaration, and it changed his life. He went on to compete in three separate winter games in the luge – Calgary in 1988, Albertville in 1992, and Salt Lake City in 2002. And he's currently training for the 2006 Torino Winter Olympics, where he will be 43 years old, competing against athletes half his age.

Principle 5

Believe in Yourself

> You weren't an accident. You weren't mass
> produced. You aren't an assembly-line product.
> You were deliberately planned, specifically gifted,
> and lovingly positioned on the Earth by
> the Master Craftsman.
>
> **Max Lucado** – Best-selling author

If you are going to be successful in creating the life of your dreams, you have to believe that you are capable of making it happen. You have to believe you have the right stuff, that you are able to pull it off. You have to believe in yourself. Whether you call it self-esteem, self-confidence, or self-assurance, it is a deep-seated belief that you have what it takes – the abilities, inner resources, talents, and skills to create your desired results.

Believing in Yourself Is an Attitude

Believing in yourself is a choice. It is an attitude you develop over time. Although it helps if you had positive and supportive parents, the fact is that most of us had run-of-the-mill parents who inadvertently passed on to us the same limiting beliefs and negative conditioning they grew up with.

But remember, the past is the past. There is no payoff for blaming them for your current level of self-confidence. It's now *your* responsibility to take charge of your own self-concept and your beliefs. You must choose to believe that you can do anything you set your mind to – anything at all – because, in fact, you can. It might help you to know that the latest brain research now indicates that with enough positive self-talk and positive visualization combined with the proper training, coaching, and practice, anyone can learn to do almost anything.

Of the hundreds of supersuccessful people I have interviewed for this and other books, almost every one of them told me, "I was not the most gifted or talented person in my field, but I chose to believe anything was possible. I studied, practiced, and worked harder than the others, and that's how I got to where I am." If a 20-year-old Texan can take up the luge and become an Olympic athlete, a college dropout can become a billionaire, and a dyslexic student who failed three grades can become a best-selling author and television producer, then you, too, can accomplish anything if you will simply believe it is possible.

If you assume in favor of yourself and act as if it is possible, then you will do the things that are necessary to bring about the result. If you believe it is impossible, you will not do what is necessary, and you will not produce the result. It becomes a self-fulfilling prophecy.

The Choice of What to Believe Is Up to You

Stephen J. Cannell failed first, fourth, and tenth grades. He couldn't read and comprehend like other kids in his class could. He would spend 5 hours with his mother studying for a test and then fail it. When he asked his friend who got an A how long he had studied for the test, he replied, "I didn't." Stephen concluded that he just wasn't intelligent.

"But I simply decided, as an act of will, to put it out of my mind," he told me. "I simply refused to think about it. Instead I focused my energies on what I was good at, and that was football. If it hadn't been for football, which I excelled at, I don't know what would have happened to me. I got my self-esteem from playing sports."

Putting all his energy into football, he earned interscholastic honors as a running back. From football, he learned that if he applied himself, he could achieve excellence.

Later he was able to transfer that belief in himself to his career, which oddly enough turned out to be writing scripts for television. Eventually he formed his own production studio, where he created, produced, and wrote over 350 scripts for 38 different shows, including *The A-Team, The Rockford Files, Baretta, 21 Jump Street, The Commish, Renegade*, and *Silk Stalkings*. At the height of his studio career, he had over 2,000 people on his payroll.

And if that isn't enough, after he sold his studio he went on to write 11 best-selling novels.

Stephen is a prime example of the fact that it is not what life hands you but how you respond to it, mentally and physically, that matters most.

> I am looking for a lot of men who have an infinite capacity to not know what can't be done.
>
> Henry Ford

You Have to Give Up "I Can't"

> The phrase "I can't" is the most powerful force of negation in the human psyche.
>
> Paul R. Scheele – Chairman, Learning Strategies Corporation

If you are going to be successful, you need to give up the phrase "I can't" and all of its cousins, such as "I wish I were able to." The words *I can't* actually disempower you. They actually make you weaker when you say them. In my seminars, I use a technique called kinesiology to test people's muscle strength as they say different phrases. I have them put their left arm out to their side, and I push down on it with my left hand to see what their normal strength is. Then I have them pick something they think they can't do, such as *I can't play the piano*, and say it out loud. I then push down on their arm again. It is always weaker.

Then I have them say, "I can do it," and their arm is stronger.

Your brain is designed to solve any problem and reach any goal that you give it. The words you think and say actually affect your body. We see that in toddlers. When you were a toddler, there was no stopping you. You thought you could climb up on anything. No barrier was too big for you to attempt to overcome. But little by little, your sense of invincibility is conditioned out of you by the emotional and physical abuse that you receive from your family, friends, and teachers, until you no longer believe you can.

You must take responsibility for removing *I can't* from your vocabulary. In the '80s, I attended a Tony Robbins seminar in which we learned to walk on burning coals. When we began, we were all afraid that we would not be able to do it – that we would burn the soles of our feet. As part of the seminar, Tony had us write down every other *I can't* that we had – *I can't find the perfect job, I can't be a millionaire, I can't find the perfect mate* – and then we threw them onto the burning coals and watched them go up in flames. Two hours later, 350 of us walked on the burning coals without anybody getting burned. That night we all learned that just like the belief that we couldn't walk on burning coals without getting burned was a lie, every other limiting belief about our abilities was also a lie.

Don't Waste Your Life Believing You Can't

In 1977, in Tallahassee, Florida, Laura Shultz, who was 63 at the time, picked up the back end of a Buick to get it off her grandson's arm. Before that time, she had never lifted anything heavier than a 50-pound bag of pet food.

Dr. Charles Garfield, author of *Peak Performance* and *Peak Performers*, interviewed her after reading about her in the *National Enquirer*. When he got to her home, she kept resisting any attempts to talk about what she called "the event." She kept asking Charlie to eat breakfast and call her Granny, which he did.

Finally he got her to talk about "the event." She said she didn't like to think about it because it challenged her beliefs about what she could and couldn't do, about what was possible. She said, "If I was able to do this when I didn't think I could, what does that say about the rest of my life? Have I wasted it?"

Charlie convinced her that her life was not yet over and that she could still do whatever she wanted to do. He asked her what she wanted to do, what her passion was. She said she had always loved rocks. She had wanted to study geology, but her parents hadn't had enough money to send both her and her brother to college, so her brother had won out.

At 63, with a little coaching from Charlie, she decided to go back to school to study geology. She eventually got her degree and went on to teach at a local community college.

Don't wait until you are 63 to decide that you can do anything you want. Don't waste years of your life. Decide that you are capable of doing anything you want and start working toward it now.

Encumbered by a low self-image,
Bob takes a job as a speed bump.

It's All About Attitude

When baseball great Ty Cobb was 70, a reporter asked him, "What do you think you'd hit if you were playing these days?"

Cobb, who had a lifetime batting average of .367, said, "About .290, maybe .300."

The reporter replied, "That's because of the travel, the night games, the artificial turf, and all the new pitches like the slider, right?"

"No," said Cobb, "it's because I am seventy."

Now that's believing in yourself!

Don't Assume You Need a College Degree

Here's another statistic showing that belief in yourself is more important than knowledge, training, or schooling: 20% of America's millionaires never set foot in college, and 21 of the 222 Americans listed as billionaires in 2003 never got their college diplomas; *2 never even finished high school!* So although education and a commitment to lifelong learning are essential to success, a formal degree isn't a requirement. This is true even in the high-tech world of the Internet. Larry Ellison, CEO of Oracle, dropped out of the University of Illinois and at the time of this writing was worth $18 billion. And Bill Gates dropped out of Harvard and later founded Microsoft. Today he is considered one of the richest men in the world, with a net worth of over $46 billion.

Even Vice President Dick Cheney dropped out of college. When you realize that the vice president, the richest man in America, and many $20 million-a-movie actors, as well as many of our greatest musicians and athletes, are all college dropouts, you see that you can start from anywhere and create a successful life for yourself.[1]

What Others Think About You Is None of Your Business

> You have to believe in yourself when no one else does. That's what makes you a winner.
>
> **Venus Williams** – Olympic gold medalist and professional tennis champion

If having others believing in you and your dream was a requirement for success, most of us would never accomplish anything. You need to base your decisions about what *you* want to do on *your* goals and desires – not the goals, desires, opinions, and judgments of your parents, friends, spouse, children, and coworkers. Quit worrying what other people think about you and follow your heart.

I like Dr. Daniel Amen's 18/40/60 Rule: When you're 18, you worry about what everybody is thinking of you;

when you're 40, you don't give a darn what anybody thinks of you; when you're 60, you realize nobody's been thinking about you at all.

Surprise, surprise! Most of the time, nobody's thinking about you at all! They are too busy worrying about their own lives, and if they are thinking about you at all, they are wondering what you are thinking about them. People think about themselves, not you. Think about it – all the time you are wasting worrying about what other people think about your ideas, your goals, your clothes, your hair, and your home could all be better spent on thinking about and doing the things that will achieve your goals.

Principle 6

Become an Inverse Paranoid

I've always been the opposite of a paranoid. I operate as if everyone is part of a plot to enhance my well-being.

Stan Dale – Founder of the Human Awareness Institute and author of *Fantasies Can Set You Free*

My earliest mentor, W. Clement Stone, was once described as an inverse paranoid. Instead of believing the world was plotting to do him harm, he chose to believe the world was plotting to do him good. Instead of seeing every difficult or challenging event as a negative, he saw it for what it could be – something that was meant to enrich him, empower him, or advance his causes.

What an incredibly positive belief!

Imagine how much easier it would be to succeed in life if you were constantly expecting the world to support you and bring you opportunity.

Successful people do just that.

In fact, there is growing research that the vibrations of positive expectation that successful people give off actually attract to them the very experiences they believe they are going to get.

Suddenly, obstacles and negatives are seen not as just another example of "Gee, the world hates me," but as opportunities to grow and change and succeed. If your car suddenly breaks down on the side of the road, instead of imagining a serial rapist pulling over to take advantage of you, think of the possibility that the guy who stops to help you will be the man you fall in love with and marry. If your company downsizes you out of a job, suddenly the chances are good that you'll find your dream job with more opportunity at much better pay. If you develop cancer, the possibility exists that in the process of reorganizing your life to effect a cure, you'll create a more healthy balance in your life and rediscover what's important to you.

Think about it.

Was there a time in your life when something terrible happened that later became a blessing in disguise?

Every negative event contains within it the seed of an equal or greater benefit.

Napoleon Hill – Author of the success classic *Think and Grow Rich*

The big blessing for me came in the 1970s when they closed the Job Corps Center in Clinton, Iowa, where I worked as a curriculum development specialist pioneering radical new learning systems for teaching underachieving students. I had unlimited support from the administration, I was working with an exciting team of bright young people who shared the same vision of making a difference, and I really enjoyed my work.

Then, out of the blue, the government decided to relocate the center. It meant I would lose my job for at least 6 months. At first I was upset at the decision, but while attending a workshop at the W. Clement & Jesse V. Stone Foundation in Chicago, I shared my predicament with the leader, who happened to be the vice president of the foundation. As a result, he offered me a job. "We'd love to have someone like you who has experience with inner-city black and Hispanic kids. Come work for us." They gave me more money, an unlimited budget, the ability to attend any workshop, training, or convention that I wanted – and I was now working directly with W. Clement Stone, who had introduced me to these success principles to begin with.

And yet, when they first announced the relocation of the Job Corps Center and my being laid off, I was angry, scared, and despondent. I thought it was the end of the world. I thought it was a bad thing. Instead, it turned out to be the major turning point of my life. In less than 3 months, my life had gone from good to great. For 2 years, I worked with some of the most amazing people I have ever met before I left to enter a doctoral program in psychological education at the University of Massachusetts.

Now, when anything "bad" happens, I remember that *everything* that ever happens to me has within it the seed of something better. I look for the upside rather than the downside. I ask myself, "Where's the greater benefit in this event?"

I'm sure that you, too, can think back to several times in your life when you thought what had happened was the end of the world – you flunked a class, lost your job, got divorced, experienced the death of a friend or a business failure, had a catastrophic injury or illness, your house burned down – and later you realized it was a blessing in disguise. The trick is to realize that whatever you are going through now is going to turn out better in the future as well. So look for the lemonade in the lemons. The more you begin to look for the good, the sooner and more often you will find it. And if you take the attitude that it is coming, the less upset and discouraged you'll get while you're waiting for it.

How Do I Use This Experience to My Advantage?

> When life hands you a lemon,
> squeeze it and make lemonade.
>
> **W. Clement Stone** – Self-made multimillionaire
> and former publisher of *Success Magazine*

Captain Jerry Coffee was a pilot who was shot down during the Vietnam War. He spent 7 years as a prisoner of war in some of the most hellish conditions known to humankind. He was beaten, became malnourished, and was kept in solitary confinement for years. But if you ask him how he feels about that experience, he would tell you that it was the most powerful transformational experience of his life. As he entered his cell for the first time, he realized he would be spending a lot of time alone. He asked himself, *How can I use this experience to my advantage?* He told me that he decided to see it as an opportunity rather than as a tragedy – an opportunity to get to know both himself and God – the only two beings he'd be spending time with – better.

Captain Coffee spent many hours each day reviewing every interaction he had ever had with anyone in his life. Slowly he began to see the patterns of what had worked and what hadn't worked in his life. Over time, he slowly psychoanalyzed himself. Eventually he came to totally know himself at the deepest levels. He fully accepted every aspect of his being, developed a profound sense of compassion for himself and all of humanity, and came to fully understand his true nature. As a result, he is one of the most wise, humble, and peaceful men I have ever met. He literally radiates love and spirituality. Though he admits that he would never want to have to do it again, he also says that he would not trade his experience as a prisoner of war for anything, for it has made him who he is today – a deeply spiritual and happy family man, a successful author, and one of the most moving inspirational speakers you could ever hope to hear.

Look for the Opportunity in Everything

What if you, too, were to greet every interaction in your life with the question "What's the potential opportunity that this is?" The supersuccessful approach every experience as an opportunity. They enter every conversation with the idea that something good will come from it. And they know that what they seek and expect, they will find.

If you take the approach that "good" is not an accident – that everyone and everything that shows up in your life is there for a reason – and that the universe is moving you toward your ultimate destiny for learning, growth, and achievement, you'll begin to see every event – no matter how difficult or challenging – as a chance for enrichment and advancement in your life.

Make a small sign or poster with the words *What's the opportunity that this is?* and put it on your desk or above your computer, so you will be constantly reminded to look for the good in every event.

You might also want to start each day by repeating the phrase, "I believe the world is plotting to do me good today. I can't wait to see what it is." And then look for the opportunities and the miracles.

He Saw the Opportunity

Mark Victor Hansen, my partner and coauthor on all of the *Chicken Soup for the Soul®* books, sees every encounter as an opportunity. He teaches everyone to say, "I'd like to be your partner on that. I can see many ways to expand your idea, reach more people, sell more, and make more money." That's how he became my partner on the *Chicken Soup* books. We were having breakfast one day, and he asked me, "What are you up to? What are you excited about?" I told him that I had decided to take all of the motivational and inspirational stories that I had been using in my talks and put them into a book without all of the other prescriptions for living that most self-help books contained. It would just be a book of stories that people could use in any way they wanted. After I described the book to him, he said, "I want to be your partner on this book. I want to help you write it."

I replied, "Mark, the book is already half written. Why would I let you be my partner at this stage of the project?"

"Well," he replied, "a lot of the stories you tell, you learned from me. I have a lot more you have never heard, I know I can get great stories from lots of other motivational speakers, and I can help you market the book to people and places you've probably never even thought of."

As we continued to talk, I realized Mark would be a great asset to the project. He is the consummate salesperson, and his dynamic energy and tireless promotional style would be a huge plus. So we struck a deal. That one conversation has been worth tens of millions in book royalties and licensing income to Mark.

You see, when you approach every encounter as an opportunity, you treat it like an opportunity. Mark saw my book project – as he sees every project he encounters – as an opportunity, and he approached the conversation from that perspective. The result has been a wonderful and profitable 12-year business relationship for both of us.

God Must Have Something Better in Store for Me

In 1987, along with 412 other people, I applied to the state government to be part of the 30-member California State Task Force to Promote Self-Esteem and Personal and Social Responsibility. Fortunately, I was selected; however, my longtime friend Peggy Bassett, the popular minister of a 2,000-member church, was not. I was surprised because I thought she would have been a perfect member. When I asked her how she felt about not being selected, she answered with a phrase that has stuck with me. I have since used it many times in my own life. She smiled and said, "Jack, I feel fine about it. It just means that *God has something better in store for me.*" She knew in her heart of hearts that she was always being led to the right experiences for her. Her positive expectancy and her certainty that all was in divine order were an inspiration to everyone who knew her. That's why her church had grown so large. It was one of the core principles of her success.

Unleash the Power of Goal-Setting

If you want to be happy, set a goal that commands your thoughts, liberates your energy, and inspires your hopes.

Andrew Carnegie – The richest man in America in the early 1900s

Once you know your life purpose, determine your vision, and clarify what your true needs and desires are, you have to convert them into specific, measurable goals and objectives and then act on them with the certainty that you will achieve them.

Experts on the science of success know the brain is a goal-seeking organism. Whatever goal you give to your subconscious mind, it will work night and day to achieve.

How Much, by When?

To make sure a goal unleashes the power of your subconscious mind, it must meet two criteria. It must be stated in a way that you and anybody else could measure it. *I will lose 10 pounds* is not as powerful as *I will weigh 135 pounds by 5 pm on June 30*. The second is clearer, because anybody can show up at 5 o'clock on June 30 and look at the reading on your scale. It will either be 135 pounds or less or not. Notice that the two criteria are *how much* (some measurable quantity such as pages, pounds, dollars, square feet, or points) and *by when* (a specific time and date).

Be as specific as possible with all aspects of your goals – include the make, model, color, year, and features … the size, weight, shape, and form … and any other details. Remember, vague goals produce vague results.

A Goal Versus a Good Idea

When there are no criteria for measurement, it is simply something you want, a wish, a preference, a *good idea*. To engage your subconscious mind, a goal or objective has to be measurable. Here are a few examples to give you more clarity:

Good Idea	Goal or Objective
I would like to own a nice home	I will own a 4,000-square-foot house on the ocean on Pacific Coast Highway in Malibu, California, by noon, April 30, 2007
I want to lose weight	I will weigh 185lb by 5 pm, January 1, 2006
I need to treat my employees better	I will acknowledge a minimum of six employees for their contribution to the department by 5 pm this Friday

Write It Out in Detail

One of the best ways to get clarity and specificity on your goals is to write them out in detail – as if you were writing specifications for a work order. Think of it as a request to God or to the universal mind. Include every possible detail.

If there is a certain house you want to own, write down its specifics in vivid colorful detail – the location, landscaping, furniture, artwork, sound system, and floor plan. If a picture of the house is available, get a copy of it. If it's an ideal fantasy, take the time to close your eyes and fill in all of the details. Then provide a date by which you expect to own it.

When you write it all down, your subconscious mind will know what to work on. It will know which opportunities to hone in on to help you reach your goal.

LOOK, LADY – YOU'RE THE ONE WHO ASKED FOR A FAMOUS MOVIE STAR WITH DARK HAIR, STRONG NOSE AND DEEP SET EYES...

You Need Goals That Stretch You

When you create your goals, be sure to write down some big ones that will stretch you. It pays to have goals that will require you to grow to achieve them. It's a good thing to have some goals that make you a little uncomfortable. Why? Because the ultimate goal, in addition to achieving your material goals, is to become a *master* at life. And to do this, you will need to learn new skills, expand your vision of what's possible, build new relationships, and learn to overcome your fears, considerations, and roadblocks.

Create a Breakthrough Goal

In addition to turning every aspect of your vision into a measurable goal, and all the quarterly and weekly and daily goals that you routinely set, I also encourage you to set what I call a breakthrough goal that would represent a quantum leap for you and your career. Most goals represent incremental improvements in our life. They are like plays that gain you 4 yards in the game of football. But what if you could come out on the first play of the game and throw a 50-yard pass? That would be a quantum leap in your progress. Just as there are plays in football that move you far up the field in one move, there are plays in life that will do the same thing. They include things such as losing 60 pounds, writing a book, publishing an article, getting on *Oprah*, winning a gold medal at the Olympics, creating a killer Web site, getting your master's or doctoral degree, getting licensed, opening your own spa, getting elected president of your union or professional association, or hosting your own radio show. The achievement of that one goal would change everything.

Wouldn't that be a goal worth pursuing with passion? Wouldn't that be something to focus on a little each day until you achieved it?

If you were an independent sales professional and knew you could get a better territory, a substantial bonus commission, and maybe even a promotion once you landed a certain number of customers, wouldn't you work day and night to achieve that goal?

If you were a stay-at-home mom whose entire lifestyle and finances would change if you earned an extra $1,000 a month through participating in a network marketing company, wouldn't you pursue every possible opportunity until you achieved that goal?

That's what I mean by a breakthrough goal. Something that changes your life, brings you new opportunities, gets you in front of the right people, and takes every activity, relationship, or group you're involved in to a higher level.

What would a breakthrough goal be for you? My youngest brother, Taylor, is a special-education teacher in Florida. He just completed a 5-year process to get his school administrator's credential, which over time will ultimately mean almost an additional $25,000 a year in income for him. That's a major leap that will significantly increase his salary and his level of influence in the school system!

Writing a best-selling book was a breakthrough goal for me and Mark Victor Hansen. *Chicken Soup for the Soul*® took us from being known in a couple of narrow fields to being recognized internationally. It created greater demand for our audio programs, speeches, and seminars. The additional income it produced allowed us to improve our lifestyle, secure our retirement, hire more staff, take on more projects, and have a larger impact in the world.

Reread Your Goals Three Times a Day

Once you've written down all your goals, both large and small, the next step on your journey to success is to activate the creative powers of your subconscious mind by reviewing your list two or three times every day. Take time to read your list of goals. Read the list (out loud with passion and enthusiasm if you are in an appropriate place) one goal at a time. Close your eyes and picture each goal as if it were already accomplished. Take a few more seconds to feel what you would feel if you had already accomplished each goal.

Following this daily discipline of success will activate the power of your desire. It increases what psychologists refer to as "structural tension" in your brain. Your brain wants to close the gap between your current reality and the vision of your goal. By constantly repeating and visualizing your goal as already achieved, you will be increasing this structural tension. This will increase your motivation, stimulate your creativity, and heighten your awareness of resources that can help you achieve your goal.

Make sure to review your goals at least twice a day – in the morning upon awakening, and again at night before going to bed. I write each of mine on a 3"× 5" index card. I keep the pack of cards next to my bed and then I go through the cards one at a time in the morning and again at night. When I travel, I take them with me.

Put a list of your goals in your daily planner or your calendar system. You can also create a pop-up or screen saver on your computer that lists your goals. The objective is to constantly keep your goals in front of you.

When Olympic decathlon gold medalist Bruce Jenner asked a roomful of Olympic hopefuls if they had a list of written goals, everyone raised their hands. When he asked how many of them had that list with them right that moment, only one person raised their hand. That person was Dan O'Brien. And it was Dan O'Brien who went on to win the gold medal in the decathlon at the 1996 Olympics in Atlanta. Don't underestimate the power of setting goals and constantly reviewing them.

Create a Goals Book

Another powerful way to speed up the achievement of your goals is to create a Goals Book. Buy a three-ring binder, a scrapbook or an 8½" × 11" journal. Then create a separate page for each of your goals. Write the goal at the top of the page and then illustrate it with pictures, words, and phrases that you cut out of magazines, catalogues, and travel brochures that depict your goal as already achieved. As new goals and desires emerge, simply add them to your list and your Goals Book. Review the pages of your Goals Book every day.

Carry Your Most Important Goal in Your Wallet

When I first started working for W. Clement Stone, he taught me to write my most important goal on the back of my business card and carry it in my wallet at all times. Every time I would open my wallet, I would be reminded of my most important goal.

When I met Mark Victor Hansen, I discovered that he, too, used the same technique. After finishing the first *Chicken Soup for the Soul®* book, we wrote "I am so happy selling 1.5 million copies of *Chicken Soup for the Soul®* by December 30, 1994." We then signed each other's cards and carried them in our wallets. I still have mine in a frame behind my desk.

Though our publisher laughed and told us we were crazy, we went on to sell 1.3 million copies of the book by our target date. Some might say, "Well, you missed your goal by 200,000 copies." Perhaps, but not by much ... and that book went on to sell well over 8 million copies in over 30 languages around the world. Believe me ... I can live with that kind of "failure."

One Goal Is Not Enough

If you are bored with life, if you don't get up every morning with a burning desire to do things – you don't have enough goals.

Lou Holtz – The only coach in NCAA history to ever lead six different college teams to postseason bowl games, and a man who also won a national championship and "coach of the year" honors

Lou Holtz, the legendary football coach of Notre Dame, is also a legendary goal-setter. His belief in goal-setting comes from a lesson he learned in 1966 when he was only 28 years old and had just been hired as an assistant coach at the University of South Carolina. His wife, Beth, was 8 months pregnant with their third child and Lou had spent every dollar he had on a down payment on a house. One month later, the head coach who had hired Lou re-signed, and Lou found himself without a job.

In an attempt to lift his spirits, his wife gave him a book

– *The Magic of Thinking Big*, by David Schwartz. The book said that you should write down all the goals you want to achieve in your life. Lou sat down at the dining-room table, turned his imagination loose, and before he knew it, he had listed 107 goals he wanted to achieve before he died. These goals covered every area of his life and included having dinner at the White House, appearing on the *Tonight Show* with Johnny Carson, meeting the pope, coaching at Notre Dame, leading his team to a national championship, and shooting a hole in one in golf. So far Lou has achieved 81 of those goals, including shooting a hole in one – not once, but twice!

Take the time to make a list of 101 goals you want to achieve in your life. Write them in vivid detail, noting where, when, how much, which model, what size, and so on. Put them on 3"×5" cards, on a goals page, or in a Goals Book. Every time you achieve one of your goals, check it off and write *victory* next to it. I made a list of 101 major goals that I wanted to achieve before I died, and I have already achieved 58 of them in only 14 years, including traveling to Africa, flying in a glider, learning to ski, attending the summer Olympic games, and writing a children's book.

Bruce Lee's Letter

Bruce Lee, arguably the greatest martial artist to have ever lived, also understood the power of declaring a goal. If you ever get a chance to visit Planet Hollywood in New York City, look for the letter hanging on the wall that Bruce Lee wrote to himself. It is dated January 9, 1970, and it is stamped "Secret." Bruce wrote, "By 1980 I will be the best known Oriental movie star in the United States and will have secured $10 million dollars. ... And in return I will give the very best acting I could possibly give every single time I am in front of the camera and I will live in peace and harmony."

Bruce made three films, and then in 1973 filmed *Enter the Dragon*, which was released that same year after his untimely death at age 33. The movie was a huge success and achieved worldwide fame for Bruce Lee.

Write Yourself a Check

Around 1990, when Jim Carrey was a struggling young Canadian comic trying to make his way in Los Angeles, he drove his old Toyota up to Mulholland Drive. While sitting there looking at the city below and dreaming of his future, he wrote himself a check for $10 million, dated it Thanksgiving 1995, added the notation "for acting services rendered," and carried it in his wallet from that day forth. The rest, as they say, is history. Carrey's optimism and tenacity eventually paid off, and by 1995, after the huge box office success of *Ace Ventura: Pet Detective*, *The Mask*, and *Dumb & Dumber*, his asking price had risen to $20 million per picture. When Carrey's father died in 1994, he placed the $10 million check into his father's coffin as a tribute to the man who had both started and nurtured his dreams of being a star.

Considerations, Fears, and Roadblocks

It's important to understand that as soon as you set a goal, three things are going to emerge that stop most people – but not you. If you know that these three things are part of the process, then you can treat them as what they are – just things to handle – rather than letting them stop you.

These three obstacles to success are *considerations*, *fears*, and *roadblocks*.

Think about it. As soon as you say you want to double your income next year, within moments considerations such as *I'll have to work twice as hard* or *I won't have time for my family* or *My wife's going to kill me* begin to emerge. You might have thoughts such as *My territory is maxed out – I can't see how I could possibly get the buyers on my current route to buy any more product from me*. If you say you're going to run a marathon, you might hear a voice in your head say, *You could get hurt*, or *You'll have to get up two hours earlier every day*. It might even suggest that you're too old to start running. These thoughts are called *considerations*. They are all the reasons why you should- n't attempt the goal – all the reasons why it is impossible.

But surfacing these considerations is a good thing. They are how you have been subconsciously stopping yourself all along. Now that you have brought them into conscious awareness, you can deal with them, confront them, and move past them.

Fears, on the other hand, are feelings. You may experience a fear of rejection, a fear of failure, or a fear of making a fool of yourself. You might be afraid of getting physically or emotionally hurt. You might be afraid that you will lose all the money you have already saved. These fears are not unusual. They are just part of the process.

Finally, you'll become aware of *roadblocks*. These are purely external circumstances – well beyond just thoughts and feelings in your head. A roadblock may be that nobody wants to join you on your project. A roadblock might be that you don't have all the money you need to move forward. Perhaps you need other investors. Roadblocks might be that your state or national government has rules or laws that prohibit what you want to do. Maybe you need to petition the government to change the rules.

Stu Lichtman, a business turnaround expert, took over a well-known shoe company in Maine that was in such bad shape financially, it was virtually doomed to go out of business. The business owed millions of dollars to creditors and was short the $2 million needed to pay them. As part of the proposed turnaround, Stu negotiated the sale of an unused plant near the Canadian border that would bring the company $600,000. But the state of Maine had a lien on the plant that would have taken all of the proceeds.

So Stu went to the governor of Maine to inform him of the company's dilemma. "We can either go bankrupt," he said, "in which case nearly one thousand Maine residents will soon be out of work and on the unemployment rolls, costing the government millions of dollars." Or the company and the government could together pursue Stu's plan of keeping the company alive, helping to keep the state's economy going, keeping nearly 1,000 people employed, and turning the company around in preparation for a takeover by another company. But the only way to achieve that goal was to overcome – you guessed it – the *roadblock* of the state's lien on the plant. Instead of letting that lien stop him, Stu decided to talk to the person who could remove the roadblock. In the end, the governor decided to cancel the lien.

Of course, you may not encounter roadblocks that require you to approach a governor – but then again, depending on how large your goal is, you very well might!

Roadblocks are simply obstacles that the world throws at you – it rains when you're trying to put on an outdoor concert, your wife doesn't want to move to Kentucky, you don't have the financial backing you need, and so on. Roadblocks are simply real-world circumstances that you need to deal with in order to move forward. They simply exist out there and always will.

Unfortunately, when these considerations, fears, and roadblocks come up, most people see them as a stop sign. They say, "Now that I'm thinking that, feeling this, and finding out about that, I think I won't pursue this goal after all." But I'm telling you not to see considerations, fears, and roadblocks as stop signs but rather as a normal part of the process that will always appear. When you re-model your kitchen, you resign yourself to a little dust and disturbance as part of the price you will have to pay. You simply learn to deal with it. The same is true of considerations, fears, and roadblocks. You just learn to deal with them.

In fact, they're supposed to appear. If they don't, it means you haven't set a goal that's big enough to stretch you and grow you. It means there's no real potential for self-development.

I always welcome considerations, fears, and roadblocks when they appear, because many times they are the very things that have been holding me back in life. Once I can see these subconscious thoughts, feelings, and obstacles, once I am aware of them, I can face them, process them, and deal with them. When I do, I become better prepared for the next venture I want to undertake.

Mastery Is the Goal

> You want to set a goal that is big enough that in the process of achieving it you become someone worth becoming.
>
> **Jim Rohn** – Self-made millionaire, success coach, and philosopher

Of course, the ultimate benefit of overcoming these considerations, fears, and roadblocks is not the material rewards that you enjoy but the personal development that you achieve in the process. Money, cars, houses, boats, attractive spouses, power, and fame can all be taken away – sometimes in the blink of an eye. But what can never be taken away is who you have become in the process of achieving your goal.

To achieve a big goal, you are going to have to become a bigger person. You are going to have to develop new skills, new attitudes, and new capabilities. You are going to have to stretch yourself, and in so doing, you will be stretched forever.

On October 20, 1991, a devastating fire roared through the scenic hills above Oakland and Berkeley, California, igniting one building every 11 seconds for over 10 hours, completely destroying 2,800 homes and apartments. A friend of mine who is also an author lost everything he owned, including his entire library, files full of research, and a nearly complete manuscript of a book he was writing. Though he was certainly devastated for a short period of time, he soon realized that although everything he owned was indeed lost in the fire, who he had become inside – everything he had learned and all the skills and self-confidence he had developed writing and promoting his books – was all still inside of him and could never be burned up in a fire.

You can lose the material things, but you can never lose your *mastery* – what you learn and who you become in the process of achieving your goals.

I believe that part of what we're on Earth to do is become masters of many skills. Christ was a master who turned water into wine, who healed people, who walked on water, and who calmed storms. He said that you and I, too, could do all these things *and more*. We definitely have that potential.

Even today, in a town square in Germany, stands a statue of Christ, its hands blown off during the intensive bombing of World War II. Though the townspeople could have restored the statue decades ago, they learned this more important lesson, instead placing a plaque underneath that reads "Christ hath no hands but yours." God needs our hands to complete His tasks on Earth. But to become masters and do this great work, we all have to be willing to go through the considerations, fears, and roadblocks.

Do It Now!

Take the time now before you go on to the next chapter to make a list of goals you want to accomplish. Make sure you have measurable (how much, by when) goals for every aspect of your vision. Then decide on a breakthrough goal, write it on the back of a business card, and put it in your wallet. And then create a list of 101 goals you want to achieve before you die. Being clear about your purpose, vision, and goals will put you in the top 3% of the world's achievers. To move into the top 1% of achievers, all you have to do is write down some specific action steps that will help you accomplish your goals on your daily to-do list. Then make sure to take those actions.

Think of it this way. If you are clear where you are going (goals) and you take several steps in that direction every day, you eventually have to get there. If I head north out of Santa Barbara and take five steps a day, eventually I have to end up in San Francisco. So decide what you want, write it down, review it constantly, and each day do something that moves you toward those goals.

Principle 8

Chunk It Down

The secret of getting ahead is getting started.
The secret of getting started is breaking your complex,
overwhelming tasks into small manageable tasks,
and then starting on the first one.

Mark Twain – Celebrated American author and humorist

Sometimes our biggest life goals seem so overwhelming. We rarely see them as a series of small, achievable tasks, but in reality, breaking down a large goal into smaller tasks – and accomplishing them one at a time – is exactly how any big goal gets achieved. So after you have decided what you really want and set measurable goals with specific deadlines, the next step is to determine all of the individual action steps you will need to take to accomplish your goal.

How to Chunk It Down

There are several ways to figure out the action steps you will need to take to accomplish any goal. One is to consult with people who have already done what you want to do and ask what steps they took. From their experience, they can give you all of the necessary steps as well as advice on what pitfalls to avoid. Another way is to purchase a book or manual that outlines the process. Yet another way is to start from the end and look backward. You simply close your eyes and imagine that it is now the future and you have already achieved your goal. Then just look back and see what you had to do to get to where you now are. What was the last thing you did? And then the thing before that, and then the thing before that, until you arrive at the first action you had to start with.

Remember that it is okay not to know how to do something. It's okay to ask for guidance and advice from those who do know. Sometimes you can get it free, and sometimes you have to pay for it. Get used to asking, "Can you tell me how to go about … ?" and "What would I have to do to … ?" and "How did you … ?" Keep researching and asking until you can create a realistic action plan that will get you from where you are to where you want to go.

What will you need to do? How much money will you need to save or raise? What new skills will you need to learn? What resources will you need to mobilize? Who will you need to enroll in your vision? Who will you need to ask for assistance? What new disciplines or habits will you need to build into your life?

A valuable technique for creating an action plan for your goals is called mind mapping.

Use Mind Mapping®

Mind mapping® is a simple but powerful process for creating a detailed to-do list for achieving your goal. It lets you determine what information you'll need to gather, who you'll need to talk to, what small steps you'll need to take, how much money you'll need to earn or raise, which deadlines you'll need to meet, and so on – for each and every goal.

When I began creating my first educational audio-cassette album – a breakthrough goal that led to extraordinary gains for me and my business – I used mind mapping® to help me "chunk down" that very large goal into all the individual tasks I would need to complete to produce a finished album.[1]

The original mind map® I created for my audio album is on page 100. To mind map® your own goals, follow these steps as illustrated in the example:

1. **Center circle:** In the center circle, jot down the name of your stated goal – in this case, *Create an Audio Educational Program*.
2. **Outside circles:** Next, divide the goal into the major categories of tasks you'll need to accomplish to achieve the greater goal – in this case, *Title, Studio, Topics, Audience,* and so on.
3. **Spokes:** Then, draw spokes radiating outward from each mini-circle and label each one (such as *Write Copy, Color Picture for Back Cover,* and *Arrange Lunch*). On a

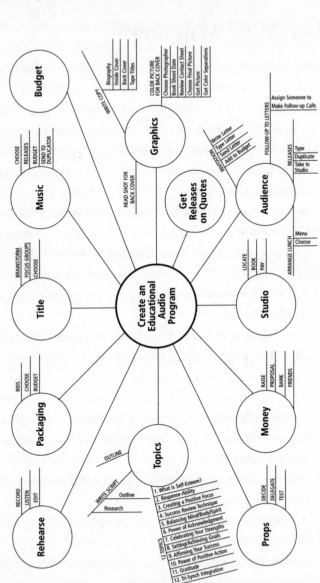

separate line connected to the minicircle, write every single step you'll need to take. Break down each one of the more detailed task spokes with action items to help you create your master to-do list.

Next, Make a Daily To-Do List

Once you've completed a mind map® for your goal, convert all of the to-do items into daily action items by listing each one on your daily to-do lists and committing to a completion date for each one. Then schedule them in the appropriate order into your calendar and do whatever it takes to stay on schedule.

Do First Things First

The goal is to stay on schedule and complete the most important item first. In his excellent book, *Eat That Frog! 21 Great Ways to Stop Procrastinating and Get More Done in Less Time*, Brian Tracy reveals not just how to conquer procrastination but also how to prioritize and complete all of your action items.

In his unique system, Brian advises goal-setters to identify the one to five things you must accomplish on any given day, and then pick the one you absolutely must do first. This becomes your biggest and ugliest frog. He then suggests you accomplish that task first – in essence, eat that frog first – and, by so doing, make the rest of your day much, much easier. It's a great strategy. But unfortunately, most of us leave the biggest and ugliest frog for last, hoping it will go away or somehow become easier. It never does. However, when you accomplish your toughest task early in the day, it sets the tone for the rest of your day. It creates momentum and builds your confidence, both of which move you farther and faster toward your goal.

Plan Your Day the Night Before

One of the most powerful tools high achievers use for chunking things down, gaining control over their life, and increasing their productivity is to plan their next day the night before. There are two major reasons why this is such a powerful strategy for success:

1. If you plan your day the night before – making a to-do list and spending a few minutes visualizing exactly how you want the day to go – your subconscious mind will work on these tasks all night long. It will think of creative ways to solve any problem, overcome any obstacle, and achieve your desired outcomes. And if we can believe some of the newer theories of quantum physics, it will also send out waves of energy that will attract the people and resources to you that you need to help accomplish your goals.[2]

2. By creating your to-do list the night before, you can start your day running. You know exactly what you're going to do and in what order, and you've already pulled together any materials you need. If you have five telephone calls to make, you would have them written down in the order you plan to make them, with the phone numbers next to the person's name and all the support materials at hand. By midmorning, you would be way ahead of most people, who waste the first half hour of the day clearing their desk, making lists, finding necessary paperwork – in short, just *getting ready* to work.

Use the Achievers Focusing System

A valuable tool that will really keep you focused on achieving all of your goals in the seven areas we explained in your vision (see pages 49–51) is the Achievers Focusing System developed by Les Hewitt of the Achievers Coaching Program. It is a form you can use to plan and hold yourself accountable for 13 weeks of goals and action steps. You can download a copy of the form and instructions on how to use it for free at www.thesuccessprinciples.com.

Principle 9

Success Leaves Clues

Success leaves clues.

Anthony Robbins – Author of *Unlimited Power*

One of the great things about living in today's world of abundance and opportunity is that almost everything you want to do has already been done by someone else. It doesn't matter whether it's losing weight, running a marathon, starting a business, becoming financially independent, triumphing over breast cancer, or hosting the perfect dinner party – someone has already done it and left clues in the form of books, manuals, audio and video programs, university classes, online courses, seminars, and workshops.

Who's Already Done What You Want to Do?

If you want to retire a millionaire, for instance, there are hundreds of books, ranging from *The Automatic Millionaire* to *The One Minute Millionaire*, and workshops ranging from Harv Eker's "Millionaire Mind" to Marshall Thurber and D.C. Cordova's "Money and You."[1] There are resources on how to make millions investing in real estate, investing in stocks, starting your own business, becoming a supersalesperson, and even marketing on the Internet.

If you want to have a better relationship with your spouse, you can read John Gray's *Men Are from Mars, Women Are from Venus*; attend a couples workshop; or take Gay and Kathlyn Hendricks' online course "The Conscious Relationship."

For virtually everything you want to do, there are books and courses on how to do it. Better yet, just a phone call away are people who've already successfully done what you want to do and who are available as teachers, facilitators, mentors, advisors, coaches, and consultants.

When you take advantage of this information, you'll discover that life is simply a connect-the-dots game, and all the dots have already been identified and organized by somebody else. All you have to do is follow the blueprint, use the system, or work the program that they provide.

Why People Don't Seek Out Clues

When I was preparing to go on a morning news show in Dallas, I asked the station's makeup artist what her long-term goals were. She said she'd always thought about opening her own beauty salon, so I asked her what she was doing to make that happen.

"Nothing," she said, "because I don't know how to go about it."

I suggested she offer to take a salon owner to lunch and ask how she had opened her own salon.

"You can do that?" the makeup artist exclaimed.

You most certainly can. In fact, you have most probably thought about approaching an expert for advice but rejected the idea with thoughts such as *Why would someone take the time to tell me what they did? Why would they teach me and create their own competition?* Banish those thoughts. You will find that most people love to talk about how they built their business or accomplished their goals.

But unfortunately, like the makeup artist in Dallas, most of us don't take advantage of all the resources available to us. There are several reasons why we don't:

- It never occurs to us. We don't see others using these resources, so we don't do it either. Our parents didn't do it. Our friends aren't doing it. Nobody where we work is doing it.
- It's inconvenient. We'd have to go to the bookstore, library, or local college. We'd have to drive across town to a meeting. We'd have to take time away from television, family, or friends.
- Asking others for advice or information puts us up against our fear of rejection. We are afraid to take the risk.
- Connecting the dots in a new way would mean change, and change – even when it is in our best interest – is

uncomfortable. Who wants to be uncomfortable?

- Connecting the dots means hard work, and frankly, most people don't want to work that hard.

Seek Out Clues

Here are three ways you can begin to seek out clues:

1. Seek out a teacher, coach, mentor; a manual, book, or audio program; or an Internet resource to help you achieve one of your major goals.
2. Seek out someone who has already done what you want to do, and ask the person if you can interview him or her for a half hour on how you should best proceed.
3. Ask someone if you can shadow them for a day and watch them work. Or offer to be a volunteer, assistant, or intern for someone you think you can learn from.

Release the Brakes

Everything you want is just outside your comfort zone.

Robert Allen – Coauthor, *The One Minute Millionaire*

Have you ever been driving your car and suddenly realized you had left the emergency brake on? Did you push down harder on the gas to overcome the drag of the brake? No, of course not. You simply released the brake … and with no extra effort you started to go faster.

Most people drive through life with their psychological emergency brake on. They hold on to negative images about themselves or suffer the effects of powerful experiences they haven't yet released. They stay in a comfort zone entirely of their own making. They maintain inaccurate beliefs about reality or harbor guilt and self-doubt. And when they try to achieve their goals, these negative images and preprogrammed comfort zones always cancel out their good intentions – no matter how hard they try.

Successful people, on the other hand, have discovered that instead of using increased willpower as the engine to power their success, it's simply easier to "release the brakes" by letting go of and replacing their limiting beliefs and changing their self-images.

Get Out of Your Comfort Zone

Think of your comfort zone as a prison you live in – a largely self-created prison. It consists of the collection of *can'ts, musts, must nots*, and other unfounded beliefs formed from all the negative thoughts and decisions you have accumulated and reinforced during your lifetime.

Perhaps you've even been *trained* to limit yourself.

Don't Be as Dumb as an Elephant

A baby elephant is trained at birth to be confined to a very small space. Its trainer will tie its leg with a rope to a wooden post planted deep in the ground. This confines the baby elephant to an area determined by the length of the rope – the elephant's comfort zone. Though the baby elephant will initially try to break the rope, the rope is too strong, and so the baby elephant learns that it can't break the rope. It learns that it has to stay in the area defined by the length of the rope.

When the elephant grows up into a 5-ton colossus that could easily break the same rope, it doesn't even try because it learned as a baby that it couldn't break the rope. In this way, the largest elephant can be confined by the puniest little rope.

Perhaps this also describes you – still trapped in a

comfort zone by something as puny and weak as the small rope and stake that controls the elephant, except your rope is made up of the limiting beliefs and images that you received and took on when you were young. If this describes you, the good news is that you can change your comfort zone. How? There are three different ways:

1. You can use affirmations and positive self-talk to affirm already having what you want, doing what you want, and being the way you want.
2. You can create powerful and compelling new internal images of having, doing, and being what you want.
3. You can simply change your behavior.

All three of these approaches will shift you out of your old comfort zone.

Stop Re-creating the Same Experience Over and Over!

An important concept that successful people understand is that you are never *stuck*. You just keep re-creating the same experience over and over by thinking the same thoughts, maintaining the same beliefs, speaking the same words, and doing the same things.

Too often, we get stuck in an endless loop of reinforcing behavior, which keeps us stuck in a constant downward spiral. Our limiting thoughts create images in our mind, and those images govern our behavior, which in turn re-inforces that limiting thought. Imagine thinking that you are going to forget your lines when you have to give a presentation at work. The thought stimulates a picture of you forgetting a key point. The image creates an experi-ence of fear. The fear clouds your clear thinking, which makes you forget one of your key points, which reinforces your self-talk that you can't speak in front of groups. *See, I knew I would forget what I was supposed to say. I can't speak in front of groups.*

As long as you keep complaining about your present circumstances, your mind will focus on it. By continually talking about, thinking about, and writing about the way things are, you are continually reinforcing those very same neural pathways in your brain that got you to where you are today. And you are continually sending out the same vibrations that will keep attracting the same people and circumstances that you have already created.

To change this cycle, you must focus instead on think-ing, talking, and writing about the reality you want to create. You must flood your unconscious with thoughts and images of this new reality.

The significant problems we face cannot be solved by the same level of thinking that created them.

Albert Einstein – Winner, Nobel Prize for Physics

What's Your Financial Temperature?

Your comfort zone works the same way the thermostat in your home works. When the temperature in the room approaches the edge of the thermal range you have set, the thermostat sends an electrical signal to the furnace or the air conditioner to turn it on or off. As the temperature in the room begins to change, the electrical signals continue to respond to the changes and keep the temperature within the desired range.

Similarly, you have an internal psychological thermostat that regulates your level of performance in the world. Instead of electrical signals, your internal performance regulator uses discomfort signals to keep you within your comfort zone. As your behavior or performance begins to approach the edge of that zone, you begin to feel uncomfortable. If what you are experiencing is outside the self-image you unconsciously hold, your body will send signals of mental tension and physical discomfort to your system. To avoid the discomfort, you unconsciously pull yourself back into your comfort zone.

My stepfather, who was a regional sales manager for NCR, noticed that each of his salespeople had a self-image of themselves as a salesperson. They were a $2,000 a month salesperson or a $3,000 a month salesperson.

If a salesperson's self-image was that he earned $3,000 a month in commissions, then whenever he earned that much in commissions in the first week of the month, he would slack off for the rest of the month.

On the other hand, if it were near the end of the month and he had only earned $1,500 in commissions, he would put in 16-hour days, work weekends, create new sales proposals, and do everything possible to get to the $3,000 level for that month.

No matter what the circumstance, a person with a $36,000 self-image would always produce a $36,000 income. To do anything else would make them uncomfortable.

I remember one year my stepfather was out selling cash registers on New Year's Eve. He was out well past midnight with the intention of selling two more cash registers so that he would qualify for the annual trip to Hawaii awarded to all salesmen who hit their yearly quota. He had earned the trip for several years running, and his self-image would not allow him to lose out that year. He sold those machines and made the trip. It would have been outside of his comfort zone to do anything less.

Imagine the same scenario in relation to your savings account. Some people are comfortable as long as they have $2,000 in their savings account. Others are uncomfortable if they have any less than 8 months' income – let's say $32,000 – salted away. Still others are comfortable with no savings and credit card debt of $25,000.

If the person needing $32,000 in savings to feel comfortable is hit with an unexpected medical expense of $16,000, he will curtail his spending, work overtime, have a garage sale – whatever it takes to get his savings back up to $32,000. Likewise, if he suddenly inherits money, he is likely to spend enough of it to stay in that $32,000 savings comfort zone.

No doubt you have heard that most lottery winners lose, spend, squander, or give away all of their newfound money within a few years of winning it. In fact, 80% of lottery winners in the United States file bankruptcy within 5 years! The reason is because they failed to develop a millionaire mind-set. As a result, they subconsciously re-create the reality that matches their previous mind-set. They feel uncomfortable with so much money, so they find some way to get back to their old familiar comfort zone.

We have a similar comfort zone for the kinds of restaurants we eat in, the hotels we stay in, the kind of car we drive, the houses we live in, the clothes we wear, the vacations we take, and the type of people we associate with.

If you have ever walked down Fifth Avenue in New York or Rodeo Drive in Beverly Hills, you have probably experienced walking into a store and immediately feeling as if you didn't belong there. The store was just too upscale for you. You felt out of place. That's your comfort zone in operation.

Change Your Behavior

When I first moved to Los Angeles in 1981, my new boss took me shopping for clothes at a very upscale men's shop in Westwood. The most I had previously ever paid for a dress shirt was $35 at Nordstrom. The cheapest shirt in this store was $95! I was stunned and broke out in a cold sweat. While my boss purchased many things that day, I bought one Italian designer shirt for $95. I was so far out of my comfort zone, I could hardly breathe. The next week, I wore the shirt and was amazed by how much better it fit, how much better it felt, and how much better I looked wearing it. After a couple more weeks of wearing it once a week, I really fell in love with it. Within a month, I bought another one. Within a year, shirts like that were all I wore. Slowly my comfort zone had changed because I'd gotten used to something better even though it cost more.

When I was on the faculty of the Million Dollar Forum and Income Builders International – two organizations dedicated to teaching people how to become millionaires – all of the trainings were held at the Ritz-Carlton Hotel in Laguna Beach, California, the Hilton Hotel on the big island of Hawaii, and other high-end luxury resort hotels. The reason was to get the participants used to being treated in a first-class way. It was part of stretching their comfort zones – changing the image of who they thought they were. Every training concluded with a black-tie dinner dance. For many of the participants, it was the first time they had ever attended a black-tie affair – another comfort zone stretch.

Change Your Self-Talk
with Affirmations

I've always believed in magic. When I wasn't doing anything in this town, I'd go up every night, sit on Mulholland Drive, look out at the city, stretch out my arms, and say, "Everybody wants to work with me. I'm a really good actor. I have all kinds of great movie offers." I'd just repeat these things over and over, literally convincing myself that I had a couple of movies lined up. I'd drive down that hill, ready to take the world on, going, "Movie offers are out there for me, I just don't hear them yet." It was like total affirmations, antidotes to the stuff that stems from my family background.[1]

Jim Carrey – Actor

One way to stretch your comfort zone is to bombard your subconscious mind with new thoughts and images – of a big bank account, a trim and healthy body, exciting work, interesting friends, memorable vacations – of all your goals as already complete. The technique you use to do this is called *affirmations*. An affirmation is a statement that describes a goal in its already completed state, such as "I am enjoying watching the sunset from the lanai of my beautiful beachfront condo on the Ka'anapali coast of Maui" or "I am celebrating feeling light and alive at my perfect body weight of one thirty-five."

The Nine Guidelines for Creating Effective Affirmations

To be effective, your affirmations should be constructed using the following nine guidelines:

1. **Start with the words *I am*.** The words *I am* are the two most powerful words in the language. The subconscious takes any sentence that starts with the words *I am* and interprets it as a command – a directive to make it happen.

2. **Use the present tense.** Describe what you want as though you already have it, as though it is already accomplished.
   Wrong: I am going to get a new red Porsche 911 Carrera.
   Right: I am enjoying driving my new red Porsche 911 Carrera.

3. **State it in the positive.** Affirm what you want, not what you don't want. State your affirmations in the positive. The unconscious does not hear the word *no*. This means that the statement "Don't slam the door" is heard as "Slam the door." The unconscious thinks in pictures, and the words "Don't slam the door" evoke a picture of slamming the door. The phrase "I am no longer afraid of flying" evokes an image of being afraid of flying,

while the phrase "I am enjoying the thrill of flying" evokes an image of enjoyment.

Wrong: I am no longer afraid of flying.

Right: I am enjoying the thrill of flying.

4. **Keep it brief**. Think of your affirmation as an advertising jingle. Act as if each word costs $1,000. It needs to be short enough and memorable enough to be easily remembered.

5. **Make it specific**. Vague affirmations produce vague results.

Wrong: I am driving my new red car.

Right: I am driving my new red Porsche 911 Carrera.

6. **Include an action word ending with -ing**. The active verb adds power to the effect by evoking an image of doing it right now.

Wrong: I express myself openly and honestly.

Right: I am confidently expressing myself openly and honestly.

7. **Include at least one dynamic emotion or feeling word**. Include the emotional state you would be feeling if you had already achieved the goal. Some commonly used words are *enjoying, joyfully, happily, celebrating, proudly, calmly, peacefully, delighted, enthusiastic, lovingly, secure, serenely,* and *triumphant*.

Wrong: I am maintaining my perfect body weight of 178 pounds.

Right: I am feeling agile and great at 178!

Note that the last one has the ring of an advertising jingle. The subconscious loves rhythm and rhymes.

That's why we are able to more easily remember things such as "Sticks and stones will break my bones, but names will never hurt me" and "*I* before *e* except after *c*, and when sounded like *a* as in *neighbor* and *weigh*."

8. **Make affirmations for yourself, not others.** When you are constructing your affirmations, make them describe your behavior, not the behavior of others.

   Wrong: I am watching Johnny clean up his room.

   Right: I am effectively communicating my needs and desires to Johnny.

9. **Add *or something better*.** When you are affirming getting a specific situation (job, opportunity, vacation), material object (house, car, boat), or relationship (husband, wife, child), always add the words "or something (someone) better." Sometimes our criteria for what we want come from our ego or from our limited experience. Sometimes there is someone or something better that is available for us, so let your affirmations include this phrase when it is appropriate.

   Example: I am enjoying living in my beautiful beachfront villa on the Ka'anapali coast of Maui or somewhere better.

A Simple Way to Create Affirmations

1. Visualize what you would like to create. See things just as you would like them to be. Place yourself inside the picture and see things through your eyes. If you want a car, see the world from inside the car as you are driving it.
2. Hear the sounds you would be hearing if you had already achieved your vision.
3. Feel the feeling you want to feel when you have created what you want.
4. Describe what you are experiencing in a brief statement, including what you are feeling.
5. If necessary, edit your affirmation to make it meet all of the above guidelines.

How to Use Affirmations and Visualization

1. Review your affirmations one to three times a day. The best times are first thing in the morning, in the middle of the day to refocus yourself, and around bedtime.
2. If appropriate, read each affirmation out loud.
3. Close your eyes and visualize yourself as the affirmation describes. See it as if you were looking out at the

scene from inside of yourself. In other words, don't see yourself standing out there in the scene; see the scene as if you were actually living it.

4. Hear any sounds you might hear when you successfully achieve what your affirmation describes – the sound of the surf, the roar of the crowd, the playing of the national anthem. Include other important people in your life congratulating you and telling you how pleased they are with your success.

5. Feel the feelings that you will feel when you achieve that success. The stronger the feelings, the more powerful the process. (If you have difficulty creating the feelings, you can affirm "I am enjoying easily creating powerful feelings in my effective work with affirmations.")

6. Say your affirmation again, and then repeat this process with the next affirmation.

Other Ways to Use Affirmations

1. Post 3" × 5" cards with your affirmations around your home.

2. Hang pictures of the things you want around your house or your room. You can put a picture of yourself in the picture.

3. Repeat your affirmations during "wasted time" such as waiting in line, exercising, and driving. You can repeat them silently or out loud.

4. Record your affirmations and listen to them while you work, drive, or fall asleep. You can use endless loop tapes, an MP3 player, or an iPod.

5. Have one of your parents record a tape of encouraging things you would like to have heard from them or words of encouragement and permission you would currently like to hear.

6. Repeat your affirmations in the first person ("I am …"), second person ("You are …"), and third person ("He/she is …").

7. Put your affirmations on your screen saver on your computer, so you'll see them every time you use your computer.

Affirmations Work

I first learned about the power of affirmations when W. Clement Stone challenged me to set a goal so far beyond my current circumstances it would literally astound me if I achieved it. Though I thought Stone's challenge had merit, I didn't really apply it to my life in a serious way until several years later when I decided to make the jump from earning $25,000 a year to making $100,000 or more.

The first thing I did was to craft an affirmation after one I'd seen by Florence Scovell Shinn. My affirmation was

God is my infinite supply and large sums of money come to me quickly and easily under the grace of God for the highest good of all concerned. I am happily and easily earning, saving, and investing $100,000 a year.

Next, I created a huge replica of a $100,000 bill, which I affixed to the ceiling above my bed. On awakening, I would see the bill, close my eyes, repeat my affirmation, and visualize what I would be enjoying if I were living a $100,000-a-year lifestyle. I envisioned the house I would live in, the furnishings and artwork I would own, the car I would drive, and the vacations I would take. I also created the feelings I would experience once I had already attained that lifestyle.

Soon I awoke one morning with my first $100,000 idea. It occurred to me that if I could sell 400,000 copies of my book, *100 Ways to Enhance Self-Concept in the Classroom*, on which I received a 25¢-per-copy royalty, I would earn a $100,000 income. I added to my morning visualizations the image of my book flying off bookstore shelves and my publisher writing me a $100,000 check. Not long after, a freelance journalist approached me and wrote an article about my work for the *National Enquirer*. As a result, thousands of additional copies of my book were sold that month.

Almost daily, more and more money-making ideas flowed into my mind. For instance, I took out small ads and sold the book on my own – making $3.00 per copy instead of just 25¢. I started a mail-order catalog of other books on self-esteem and made even more money from these same buyers. The University of Massachusetts saw my catalog and invited me to sell books at a weekend conference, helping me generate more than $2,000 in 2 days – and introducing me to another strategy for making $100,000 a year.

At the same time I was visualizing greater book sales, I also got the idea to generate more income from my workshops and seminars. When I asked a friend who did similar work how I could charge higher fees, he revealed he was *already* charging more than double what I was being paid! With his encouragement, I instantly tripled my rates and discovered the schools that were hiring me to speak had budgets even higher than that.

My affirmation was paying off big time. But if I hadn't set the goal to make $100,000 and been diligent about affirming and visualizing it, I never would have raised my speaking fees, started a mail-order bookstore, attended a major conference, or been interviewed for a major publication.

As a result, my income that year skyrocketed from $25,000 to over $92,000!

Of course, I missed my $100,000 goal by $8,000, but I can assure you I wasn't depressed about it. On the contrary, I was ecstatic. I had almost quadrupled my income in less than 1 year, using the power of visualization and affirmations coupled with the willingness to act when I had an "inspired idea."

After our $92,000 year, my wife asked me, "If affirmations worked for $100,000, do you think they would also work for $1 million?" Using affirmations and visualization, we went on to achieve that goal as well and have continued to make $1 million or more every year since.

Principle 11

See What You Want, Get What You See

*Imagination is everything. It is the
preview of life's coming attractions.*
Albert Einstein – Winner, Nobel Prize for Physics

Visualization – or the act of creating compelling and vivid
pictures in your mind – may be the most underutilized
success tool you possess because it greatly accelerates the
achievement of any success in three powerful ways.

1. Visualization activates the creative powers of your subconscious mind.
2. Visualization focuses your brain by programming its
   reticular activating system (RAS) to notice available
   resources that were always there but were previously
   unnoticed.
3. Visualization magnetizes and attracts to you the people, resources, and opportunities you need to achieve
   your goal.

When you perform any task in real life, researchers have
found, your brain uses the same identical processes it

would use if you were only vividly visualizing that activity. In other words, your brain sees no difference whatsoever between visualizing something and actually doing it.

This principle also applies to learning anything new. Harvard University researchers found that students who visualized in advance performed tasks with nearly 100% accuracy, whereas students who didn't visualize achieved only 55% accuracy.

Visualization simply makes the brain achieve more. And though none of us were ever taught this in school, sports psychologists and peak performance experts have been popularizing the power of visualization since the 1980s. Almost all Olympic and professional athletes now employ the power of visualization.

Jack Nicklaus, the legendary golfer with more than 100 tournament victories and over $5.7 million in winnings, once said, "I never hit a shot, not even in practice, without having a very sharp, in-focus picture of it in my head. It's like a color movie. First I 'see' where I want it to finish, nice and white and sitting high on the bright green grass. Then the scene quickly changes, and I 'see' the ball going there: its path, trajectory, and shape, even its behavior on landing. Then there's sort of a fade-out, and the next scene shows me making the kind of swing that will turn the previous images into reality."

How Visualization Works to Enhance Performance

When you visualize your goals as already complete each and every day, it creates a conflict in your subconscious mind between what you are visualizing and what you currently have. Your subconscious mind tries to resolve that conflict by turning your current reality into the new, more exciting vision.

This conflict, when intensified over time through constant visualization, actually causes three things to happen:

1. It programs your brain's RAS to start letting into your awareness anything that will help you achieve your goals.
2. It activates your subconscious mind to create solutions for getting the goals you want. You'll start waking up in the morning with new ideas. You'll find yourself having ideas in the shower, while you are taking long walks, and while you are driving to work.
3. It creates new levels of motivation. You'll start to notice you are unexpectedly doing things that take you to your goal. All of a sudden, you are raising your hand in class, volunteering to take on new assignments at work, speaking out at staff meetings, asking more directly for what you want, saving money for the things that you want, paying down a credit card debt, or taking more risks in your personal life.

Let's take a closer look at how the RAS works. At any one time, there are about 8 million bits of information streaming into your brain – most of which you cannot attend to, nor do you need to. So your brain's RAS filters most of them out, letting into your awareness only those signals that can help you survive and achieve your most important goals.

So how does your RAS know what to let in and what to filter out? It lets in anything that will help you achieve the goals you have set and *constantly* visualize and affirm. It also lets in anything that matches your beliefs and images about yourself, others, and the world.

The RAS is a powerful tool, but it can only look for ways to achieve the exact pictures you give it. Your creative subconscious doesn't think in words – it can only think in pictures. So how does this help your effort to become successful and achieve the life of your dreams?

When you give your brain specific, colorful, and vividly compelling pictures to manifest – it will seek out and capture all the information necessary to bring that picture into reality for you. If you give your mind a $10,000 problem, it will come up with a $10,000 solution. If you give your mind a $1 million problem, it will come up with a $1 million solution.

If you give it pictures of a beautiful home, an adoring spouse, an exciting career, and exotic vacations, it will go to work on achieving those. By contrast, if you are constantly feeding it negative, fearful, and anxious pictures – guess what? – it will achieve those, too.

The Process for Visualizing Your Future

The process of visualizing for success is really quite simple. All you have to do is close your eyes and see your goals as already complete.

If one of your objectives is to own a nice house on the lake, then close your eyes and see yourself walking through the exact house you would like to own. Fill in all of the details. What does the exterior look like? How is it landscaped? What kind of view does it have? What do the living room, kitchen, master bedroom, dining room, family room, and den look like? How is it furnished? Go from room to room and fill in all of the details.

"Don't disturb Daddy. He's busy visualizing unparalleled success in the business world and, by extension, a better life for us all."

Make the images as clear and bright as possible. This goes for any goal you make – whether it's in the area of work, play, family, personal finances, relationships, or philanthropy. Write down each of your goals and objectives, then review them, affirm them, and visualize them every day.

Then, each morning when you awake and each night before you go to bed, read through the list of goals out loud, pausing after each one to close your eyes and re-create the visual image of that completed goal in your mind. Continue through the list until you have visualized each goal as complete and fulfilled. The whole process will take between 10 and 15 minutes, depending on how many goals you have. If you meditate, do your visualization right after you finish meditating. The deepened state you have achieved in meditation will heighten the impact of your visualizations.

Adding Sounds and Feelings to the Pictures

To multiply the effect many times over, add sound, smells, tastes, and feelings to your pictures. What sounds would you be hearing, what smells would you be smelling, what tastes would you be tasting, and – most importantly – what emotions and bodily sensations would you be feeling if you had already achieved your goal?

If you were imagining your dream house on the beach, you might add in the sound of the surf lapping at the shore outside your home, the sound of your kids playing on the sand, and the sound of your spouse's voice thanking you for being such a good provider.

Then add in the feelings of pride of ownership, satisfaction at having achieved your goal, and the feeling of the sun on your face as you sit on your deck looking out over the ocean at a beautiful sunset.

Fuel Your Images with Emotion

By far, these emotions are what propel your vision forward. Researchers know that when accompanied by intense emotions, an image or scene can stay locked in the memory forever.

I'm sure you remember exactly where you were when John F. Kennedy was assassinated in 1963 or when the World Trade Center collapsed on September 11, 2001. Your brain remembers it all in great detail because not only did your brain filter information you needed for survival under these tense moments but also the images themselves were created with intense emotion. These intense emotions actually stimulate the growth of additional spiny protuberances on the dendrites of brain neurons, which ultimately creates more neural connections, thus locking in the memory much more solidly. You can bring this same emotional intensity to your own visualizations by adding inspiring music, real-life smells, deeply felt passion, even loudly shouting your affirmations with exaggerated enthusiasm. The more passion, excitement, and energy you can muster, the more powerful will be the ultimate result.

Visualization Works

Olympic gold medalist Peter Vidmar describes his use of visualization in his successful pursuit of the gold:

> To keep us focused on our Olympic goal, we began ending our workouts by visualizing our dream. We visualized ourselves actually competing in the Olympics and achieving our dream by practicing what we thought would be the ultimate gymnastics scenario.
>
> I'd say, "Okay, Tim, let's imagine it's the men's gymnastics team finals of the Olympic Games. The United States team is on its last event of the night, which just happens to be the high bar. The last two guys up for the United States are Tim Daggett and Peter Vidmar. Our team is neck and neck with the People's Republic of China, the reigning world champions, and we have to perform our routines perfectly to win the Olympic team gold medal."

At that point we'd each be thinking, *Yeah, right. We're never going to be neck and neck with those guys. They were number one at the Budapest world championships, while our team didn't even win a medal. It's never going to happen.*

But what if it did happen? How would we feel?

We'd close our eyes and, in this empty gym at the end of a long day, we'd visualize an Olympic arena with 13,000 people in the seats and another 200 million watching live on television. Then we'd practice our routines. First, I'd be the announcer. I'd cup my hands around my mouth and say, "Next up, from the United States of America, Tim Daggett." Then Tim would go through his routine as if it were the real thing.

Then Tim would go over to the corner of the gym, cup his hands around his mouth, and, in his best announcer voice, say, "Next up, from the United States of America, Peter Vidmar."

Then it was my turn. In my mind, I had one chance to perfectly perform my routine in order for our team to win the gold medal. If I didn't, we'd lose.

Tim would shout out, "Green light," and I'd look at the superior judge, who was usually our coach Mako. I'd raise my hand, and he'd raise his right back. Then

I'd turn, face the bar, grab hold, and begin my routine.

Well, a funny thing happened on July 31, 1984.

It was the Olympic Games, men's gymnastics team finals in Pauley Pavilion on the UCLA campus. The 13,000 seats were all filled, and a television audience in excess of 200 million around the world tuned in. The United States team was on its last event of the night, the high bar. The last two guys up for the United States just happened to be Tim Daggett and Peter Vidmar. And just as we visualized, our team was neck and neck with the People's Republic of China. We had to perform our high bar routines perfectly to win the gold medal.

I looked at Coach Mako, my coach for the past 12 years. As focused as ever, he simply said, "Okay, Peter, let's go. You know what to do. You've done it a thousand times, just like every day back in the gym. Let's just do it one more time, and let's go home. You're prepared."

He was right. I had planned for this moment and visualized it hundreds of times. I was prepared to perform my routine. Rather than seeing myself actually standing in the Olympic arena with 13,000 people in the stands and 200 million watching on television, in my mind I pictured myself back in the UCLA gym at the end of the day with two people left in the gym.

When the announcer said, "From the United States of America, Peter Vidmar," I imagined it was my buddy Tim Daggett saying it. When the green light came on, indicating it was time for the routine, I imagined that it wasn't really a green light but that it was Tim shouting, "Green light!" And when I raised my hand toward the superior judge from East Germany, in my mind I was signaling my coach, just like I had signaled him every day at the end of hundreds of workouts. In the gym, I always visualized I was at the Olympic finals. At the Olympic finals, I visualized I was back in the gym.

I turned, faced the bar, jumped up, and grabbed on. I began the same routine I had visualized and practiced day after day in the gym. I was in memory mode, going yet again where I'd already gone hundreds of times. I quickly made it past the risky double-release move that had harpooned my chances at the world championships. I moved smoothly through the rest of my routine and landed a solid dismount, where I anxiously waited for my score from the judges.

With a deep voice the announcement came through the speaker, "The score for Peter Vidmar is 9.95."

"Yes!" I shouted. "I did it!" The crowd cheered loudly as my teammates and I celebrated our victory.

Thirty minutes later, we were standing on the Olympic medal platform in the Olympic arena with 13,000 people in the stands and over 200 million watching on television, while the gold medals were officially draped around our necks. Tim, me, and our teammates stood proudly wearing our gold medals as the national anthem played and the American flag was raised to the top of the arena. It was a moment we visualized and practiced hundreds of times in the gym. Only this time, it was for real.

What if I Don't See Anything When I Visualize?

Some people are what psychologists refer to as *eidetic visualizers*. When they close their eyes, they see everything in bright, clear, three-dimensional Technicolor images. Most of us, however, are noneidetic visualizers. That means you don't really *see* an image as much as you just *think* it. This is perfectly okay. It still works just as well. Do the visualization exercise of imagining your goals as already complete twice a day, every day, and you will still get the same benefit as those people who claim to actually see the image.

Use Printed Pictures to Help You

If you have trouble seeing your goals, use pictures, images, and symbols you collect to keep your conscious and subconscious mind focused on your goals. For example, if one of your goals is to own a new Lexus LS-430, you can take your camera down to your local Lexus dealer and ask a salesperson to take a picture of you sitting behind the wheel.

If your goal is to visit Paris, find a poster of the Eiffel Tower – then cut out a picture of you and place it at the base of the Eiffel Tower as if it were a photograph taken of you in Paris. Several years ago I did this with a picture of the Sydney Opera House, and within a year I was in Sydney, standing in front of it.

If your goal is to be a millionaire, you might want to write yourself a check for $1,000,000 or create a bank statement that shows your bank account or your stock portfolio with a $1,000,000 balance.

Mark Victor Hansen and I created a mock-up of the *New York Times* Best-Seller List with the original *Chicken Soup for the Soul*® in the number-one spot. Within 15 months, that dream became a reality. Four years later, we made a *Guinness* world record for having seven books on the *New York Times* Best-Seller List at the same time.

Once you have created these images, you can place them – one to a page – in a three-ring binder that you review every day. Or you could make a dream board or treasure map – a collage of all these images on a bulletin board, wall, or a refrigerator door – somewhere where you will see them every day.

When NASA was working on putting a man on the moon, they had a huge picture of the moon covering the entire wall, from floor to ceiling, of their main construction area. Everyone was clear on the goal, and they reached that goal 2 years ahead of schedule!

Vision Boards and Goal Books Made Their Dreams Come True

In 1995 John Assaraf created a vision board and put it up on the wall in his home office. Whenever he saw a materialistic thing he wanted or a trip he wanted to take, he'd get a photo of it and glue it to the board. Then he'd see himself already enjoying the object of his desire.

In May 2000, having just moved into his new home in Southern California a few weeks earlier, he was sitting in his office at 7:30 am when his 5-year-old son Keenan came in and sat on a couple of boxes that had been in storage 4 years. Keenan asked his father what was in the boxes. When John told him his vision boards were in the boxes, Keenan replied, "Your vision whats?"

John opened one of the boxes to show Keenan a vision board. John smiled as he looked at the first board and saw pictures of a Mercedes sports car, a watch, and some other items, all of which he had acquired by then.

But as he pulled out the second board, he began to cry. On that board was a picture of the house he had just bought and was living in! Not a house *like* it but *the* house! The 7,000-square-foot house that sits on 6 acres of spectacular views, with a 3,000-square-foot guest house and office complex, a tennis court, and 320 orange trees – that very home was a home he had seen in a picture that he had cut out of *Dream Homes* magazine 4 years earlier!

Caryl Kristensen and Marilyn Kentz – better known as "The Mommies" because they make their living joking about kids, family life, and the stresses of motherhood – know the power of creating goal pictures to make their dreams come true. They started their friendship as well as their careers in the small farm town of Petaluma, California, where they were neighbors. Once they decided to become performers and create shows, they made a Goals Book, in which they listed all the things they wanted to achieve, and then illustrated them with pictures. Without exception, everything they put in the book came true!

Their achievements include *The Mommies*, an NBC sitcom that aired between 1993 and 1995, the *Caryl & Marilyn Show*, a talk show that aired on ABC between 1996 and 1997, Showtime and Lifetime cable specials, and their highly successful book, *The Mother Load*.

Because Caryl and Marilyn are both illustrators, drawing their goals seemed the easiest way to go about it, but you don't have to have drawing skills to make your own

Goals Book. They worded their goals in the present tense, added feeling phrases such as "I'm feeling content and grateful," "I feel relaxed and joyful," and "Living in this wonderful house is so much fun," and they always finished off their page with this phrase: "This or something better is manifesting itself for the good of all concerned."

And this or something better always happened.

Start Now

Set aside time each and every day to visualize every one of your goals as already complete. This is one of the most vital things you can do to make your dreams come true. Some psychologists are now claiming that one hour of visualization is worth 7 hours of physical effort. That's a tall claim, but it makes an important point – visualization is one of the strongest tools in your success toolbox. Make sure you use it.

You don't need to visualize your future achievements for a whole hour. Just 10 to 15 minutes is plenty. Azim Jamal, a prominent speaker in Canada, recommends what he calls "the Hour of Power" – 20 minutes of visualization and meditation, 20 minutes of exercise, and 20 minutes of reading inspirational or informational books. Imagine what would happen to your life if you did this every day.

Principle 12

Act As If

Believe and act as if it were impossible to fail.

Charles F. Kettering – Inventor with over 140 patents
and honorary doctorates from nearly 30 universities

One of the great strategies for success is to act as if you are *already where you want to be*. This means thinking like, talking like, dressing like, acting like, and feeling like the person who has already achieved your goal. Acting as if sends powerful commands to your subconscious mind to find creative ways to achieve your goals. It programs the reticular activating system (RAS) in your brain to start noticing anything that will help you succeed, and it sends strong messages to the universe that this end goal is something you really want.

Start Acting As If

The first time I noticed this phenomenon was at my local bank. There were several tellers working there, and I noticed that one in particular always wore a suit and tie. Unlike the other two male tellers who just wore a shirt and a tie, this young man looked like an executive.

A year later, I noticed he had been promoted to his own desk where he was taking loan applications. Two years later, he was a loan officer, and later he became the branch manager. I asked him about this one day, and he replied that he always knew he would be a branch manager, so he studied how the manager dressed and started dressing that way. He studied how the manager treated people and started interacting with people the same way. He started acting as if he were a branch manager long before he ever became one.

> To fly as fast as thought, to be anywhere there is, you must first begin by knowing that you have already arrived.
>
> **Richard Bach** – Author of *Jonathan Livingston Seagull*

Becoming an International Consultant

In the late '70s, I met a seminar leader who had just returned from Australia. I decided that I, too, wanted to travel and speak around the globe. I asked myself what I would need to become an international consultant. I called the passport office and asked them to send me an application. I purchased a clock that showed all the international time zones. I had business cards printed with the words *international consultant* on them. Finally, I decided that Australia would be the first place I would like to go, so I went to a travel agency and got a huge travel poster featuring the Sydney Opera House, Ayers Rock, and a kangaroo-crossing sign. Every morning while I ate my breakfast, I looked at that poster on my refrigerator and imagined being in Australia.

Less than a year later, I was invited to conduct seminars in Sydney and Brisbane. As soon as I started acting as if I were an international consultant, the universe responded by treating me like one – the powerful Law of Attraction at work.

The Law of Attraction simply states that like attracts like. The more you create the vibration – the mental and emotional states – of already having something, the faster you attract it to you. This is an immutable law of the universe and critical to accelerating your rate of success.

Acting As If in the PGA

Fred Couples and Jim Nantz were two kids who loved golf and had very large dreams. Fred's goal was to someday win the Masters Tournament, and Jim's was to someday work for CBS Sports as an announcer. When Fred and Jim were suitemates at the University of Houston in the late '70s, they used to playact the scene where the winner of the Masters is escorted into Butler Cabin to receive his green jacket and be interviewed by the CBS announcer. Fourteen years later, the scene they had rehearsed many times in Taub Hall at the University of Houston played out in reality as the whole world was watching. Fred Couples won the Masters and was taken by tournament officials into Butler Cabin, where he was interviewed by none other than CBS Sports announcer Jim Nantz. After the cameras stopped rolling, the two embraced each other with tears in their eyes. They always knew it was going to be the Masters that Fred won, and that Jim would be there to cover it for CBS – the amazing power of acting as if with unwavering certainty.

The Millionaire Cocktail Party

In many of my seminars we do an exercise called the Millionaire Cocktail Party. Everyone stands up and socializes with the other participants as if they were all at an actual cocktail party. However, they must act as if they have already achieved all of their financial goals in life. They act as if they already have everything they want in life – their dream house, their vacation home, their dream car, their dream career – as well as if they have achieved any personal, professional, or philanthropic goals that are important to them.

Everyone suddenly becomes more animated, alive, enthusiastic, and outgoing. People who seemed shy a few minutes earlier reach out and assertively introduce themselves to others. The energy and volume level of the room soars. People excitedly tell each other about their achievements, invite each other to their vacation homes in Hawaii and the Bahamas, and discuss their recent safaris in Africa and their philanthropic missions to Third World countries.

After about 5 minutes, I stop the exercise and ask people to share how they are feeling. People report feeling excited, passionate, positive, supportive, generous, happy, self-confident, and content.

I then ask them to look at the fact that their inner feelings – both emotional and physiological – were different, even though in reality their outer circumstances were still the same. They had not actually become millionaires in the real world, but they had begun to feel like millionaires simply by acting as if they were.

Be, Do, and Have Everything You Want … Starting Now

You can begin right now to act as if you have already achieved any goal you desire, and that outer experience of acting as if will create the inner experience – the millionaire mind-set, as it were – that will take you to the actual manifestation of that experience.

Once you choose what it is you want to be, do, or have, all you have to do is start acting as if you already are being, doing, or having it. How would you act if you already were a straight-A student, top salesperson, highly paid consultant, rich entrepreneur, world-class athlete, best-selling author, internationally acclaimed artist, sought-after speaker, or celebrated actor or musician? How would you think, talk, act, carry yourself, dress, treat other people, handle money, eat, live, travel, and so forth?

Once you have a clear picture of that, start being it – now!

Successful people exude self-confidence, ask for what they want, and say what they don't want. They think anything is possible, take risks, and celebrate their successes. They save a portion of their income and share a portion with others. You can do all of those things now before you ever become rich and successful. These things don't cost money, just intention. And as soon as you start acting as if, you will start drawing to you the very people and things that will help you achieve it in real life.

Remember, the proper order of things is to start now and *be* who you want to be, then *do* the actions that go along with being that person, and soon you will find that you easily *have* everything you want in life – health, wealth, and fulfilling relationships.

The Party That Could Change Your Life

In 1986 I attended a party given by Diana von Welanetz and the Inside Edge that deeply impacted the lives of all of us who attended. It was a "come as you will be in 1991 party" held on the *Queen Mary* in Long Beach, California. Those of us who attended were to envision where we would like to be in 1991 – 5 years into the future. After we had created our ideal vision, we were to then stretch our imaginations even further, to make our vision even bigger still.

When we attended the party, we were to act as if it really were 1991 and our vision had already come true. We were to dress the part, talk the part, and bring any props that demonstrated that our dream had already come true – books written, awards earned, and large paychecks received. We were to spend the evening bragging about our accomplishments, celebrating our successes and the successes of others, talking about how happy and fulfilled we were, and discussing what we were going to do next. We were to stay in character the entire night.

When we arrived, we were met by 20 men and women who had been hired to play the part of adoring fans and paparazzi. Cameras flashed and fans screamed our names, asking for autographs.

I went as a best-selling author with several reviews of my number-one *New York Times* best seller to show people. A man who came as a multimillionaire dressed as a beach bum – his vision of retirement – spent the evening handing out real lottery tickets to everyone at the party. A woman brought a mock edition of *Time* magazine with her face on the cover for winning an international award for making advances in the peace movement.

A man who wanted to retire and spend his life as a

sculptor showed up in a leather sculptor's apron with a hammer and chisel and safety goggles and pictures of sculptures he had made. Another gentleman who wanted to become a successful stock trader spent the entire evening answering his cell phone, talking animatedly and then commanding, "Buy five thousand shares" or "Sell ten thousand shares." He had actually hired someone to call him every 15 minutes during the party just to carry off his "act as if"!

A movie producer arrived dressed in a tuxedo, having envisioned winning an award for his first coproduction with the Russians. His wife, who was just embarking on a writing career and had yet to sell a book, arrived carrying mock-ups of three books she had written. In the spirit of everyone supporting everyone else's dream, people told her that they had seen her on *Oprah, Sally Jesse Raphael*, and the *Today* show. Others congratulated her for making the best-seller lists and for winning a Pulitzer prize. And so it went all evening long. (Many of you now know this author, Susan Jeffers, who did go on from that transformational evening to publish 17 successful books, including the internationally acclaimed best-selling classic *Feel the Fear and Do It Anyway.*)

And as you know if you've read this far, the same thing happened to me. I went on to write, compile, and edit over 80 books, including 11 number-one *New York Times* best sellers. That party, where we maintained our future personas for over 4 hours, flooded our subconscious minds with powerful images of already having achieved our aspirations. These vivid experiences, infused with the positive emotions generated by the events of the evening, strengthened the positive neural pathways in our brains that in some cases forged, and in other cases deepened, our new self-images of being supersuccessful.

But most importantly, it worked. All those who attended that party have gone on to realize the dreams they acted out that night and much, much more.

Make the commitment to throw a "come as you will be" party for your closest circle of friends, your company, your business associates, your graduating class, or your mastermind group. Why not build it into your annual convention or sales meeting? Think of the creative energy, awareness, and support it will release.

You can use the invitation on the next page:

Come as you will be
. . . in 2011

join us for a celebration that will stretch your
imagination and catapult you into your own future

When: ....

Where: ....

Given by: ....

RSVP to: ....

**Arrive as who you will be in 5 years from now.
Dress in your very best.**

Speak only in the present tense the entire evening,
as if it were already 2011, all your goals have
been achieved, and all your dreams have come true.

You will be videotaped as you arrive.
Bring props to show everyone what you have achieved
in the years between, such as best-selling books you've written,
magazine covers you've been on, awards you've won, and
photographs or scrapbooks of your achievements. Throughout
the evening, you will have the opportunity to applaud others in
their achievements and to recieve congratulations.

And the Party Continues

A few years after the party in Long Beach, I appeared on the *Caryl & Marilyn Show* on ABC and shared my experience on the *Queen Mary*. They immediately recognized the power of the idea and decided to throw a similar party for all of their crew and friends. Here is what Marilyn wrote about it 6 years later in her book *Not Your Mother's Midlife*:

I giggle whenever I think about our Five-Year Party. Caryl and I went all out with fake paparazzi, *Entertainment Tonight* interviews, and a red-carpet entrance. I had sent telegrams to the party house from famous people congratulating everyone on their accomplishments. Caryl and I carried around copies of our new *Mommy Book*. I'd made mock books with a cover using this crazy picture of us wearing plastic flamingos on our heads – the only photo I could drum up that afternoon. At that time we didn't even have an outline, let alone a book deal.

Two years later HarperCollins released our book *The Mother Load*, and by pure coincidence, out of all the head shots we submitted for the jacket, the photograph they decided to use was the same one I used on the "fake" book jacket. The book did very well – went through three hardcover printings and eventually also sold as a paperback …

Six years ago my daughter was ten and in elementary school. Because I was afraid she'd be a horrid, naughty, sassy teenager within the next five years, I hired a young fifteen-year-old to play my darling, loving, "good yet normal" teenage daughter. I provided her with a script. She burst into the house and kissed my cheek, exclaiming how great it was that we had this special relationship where we talked about everything and hardly ever fought. She said she couldn't stay long because she was on her way to a party with her designated driver and, while she was quite a healthy, normal teenager, I really had nothing to worry about because she never got carried away with drinking alcohol or smoking pot. I also had to throw this in: She explained that she was going to see Denzel Washington's son at the party. The whole bit got lots of laughs.

Fast-forward six years. First of all, my daughter and I have that special relationship I dreamed about. I don't know why, but we do talk about everything. (Okay, I'm not dumb … certain things are saved for best friends and siblings.) We rarely ever fight, she's a wise and moderate teenager, and she actually goes to parties with Denzel's son. It's true! When I'd made up that little scenario I'd had no idea if Denzel lived here in Los Angeles or in New York: I didn't even know if he had kids. What are the chances that my daughter would end up in the same high school as his son? What a crazy Five-Year Party![1]

The purpose of the "come as you will be party" is to create an emotionally charged experience of what it will be like when you have made it – when you have achieved your dreams. When you spend an evening living out the lifestyle you want and deserve, you lay down powerful blueprints in your subconscious mind that will later support you in perceiving opportunities, creating powerful solutions, attracting the right people, and taking the necessary actions to achieve your dreams and goals.

Be clear that one party like this is not enough by itself to change your entire future. You will still have to do other things to make it happen. However, it is one more piece in an overall system of powerful "acting as if" strategies that will support you in the creation of your desired future.

Principle 13

Take Action

Things may come to those who wait,
but only the things left by those who hustle.

Abraham Lincoln – Sixteenth president of the United States

What we think or what we know or what we
believe is, in the end, of little consequence.
The only consequence is what we do.

John Ruskin – English author, art critic, and social commentator

The world doesn't pay you for what you know; it pays you for what you do. There's an enduring axiom of success that says, "The universe rewards action." Yet as simple and as true as this principle is, it's surprising how many people get bogged down in analyzing, planning, and organizing when what they really need to do is take action.

When you take action, you trigger all kinds of things that will inevitably carry you to success. You let those around you know that you are serious in your intention. People wake up and start paying attention. People with similar goals become aligned with you. You begin to learn things from your experience that cannot be learned from listening to others or from reading books. You begin to get feedback about how to do it better, more efficiently, and more quickly. Things that once seemed confusing begin to become clear. Things that once appeared difficult begin to be easier. You begin to attract others who will support and encourage you. All manner of good things begin to flow in your direction once you begin to take action.

Talk Is Cheap!

Over the years of teaching and coaching people in my company and in my seminars, I have found that the one thing that seems to separate winners from losers more than anything else is that winners take action. They simply get up and do what has to be done. Once they have developed a plan, they start. They get into motion. Even if they don't start perfectly, they learn from their mistakes, make the necessary corrections, and keep taking action, all the time building momentum, until they finally produce the result they set out to produce … or something even better than they conceived of when they started.

To be successful, you have to do what successful people do, and successful people are highly action-oriented. I have already covered how to create a vision, set goals, break them down into small steps, anticipate obstacles and plan how to deal with them, visualize and affirm your success, and believe in yourself and your dreams. Now it's time to take action. Enroll in the course, get the necessary training, call the travel agent, start writing that book, start saving for the down payment on your home, join the health club, sign up for those piano lessons, or write that proposal.

Nothing Happens until You Take Action

If your ship doesn't come in, swim out to meet it.

Jonathan Winters – Grammy Award–winning comedian, actor, writer, and artist

To demonstrate the power of taking action in my seminars, I hold up a $100 bill and ask, "Who wants this $100 bill?" Invariably, most of the people in the audience will raise their hands. Some will wave their hands vigorously back and forth; some will even shout out "I want it" or "I'll take it" or "Give it to me." But I just stand there calmly holding out the bill until they *get* it. Eventually, someone jumps out of her seat, rushes to the front of the room, and takes the bill from my hand.

After the person sits down – now $100 richer for her efforts – I ask the audience, "What did this person do that no one else in the room did? She got off her butt and took action. She did what was necessary to get the money. And that is exactly what you must do if you want to succeed in life. You must take action, and, in most cases, the sooner the better." I then ask, "How many of you thought about getting up and just coming and taking the money but stopped yourselves?"

I then ask them to remember what they told themselves that stopped them from getting up.

The usual answers are

> "I didn't want to look like I wanted or needed it that badly."
> "I wasn't sure if you would really give it to me."
> "I was too far back in the room."
> "Other people need it more than I do."
> "I didn't want to look greedy."
> "I was afraid I might be doing something wrong and then people would judge me or laugh at me."
> "I was waiting for further instructions."

I then point out that whatever things they said to stop themselves are the same things that they say to stop themselves in the rest of their lives.

One of the universal truths in life is "How you do anything is how you do everything." If you are cautious here, you are probably cautious everywhere. If you hold yourself back for fear of looking foolish here, you probably hold yourself back for fear of looking foolish elsewhere. You have to identify those patterns and break through them. It's time to stop holding yourself back and just go for the gold.

Ruben Gonzalez Goes for Olympic Gold

Ever since third grade, Ruben Gonzalez had wanted to be an Olympic athlete. He respected the Olympians because they were an example of what he believed in – they are willing to commit to a goal, risk adversity in the pursuit of it, and fail and keep trying until they succeed.

But it was not until he was in college and saw Scott Hamilton compete in the 1984 Sarajevo Games that he actually made the decision to train for the Olympics. Ruben said to himself, *If that little guy can do it, I can do it too! I'm going to be in the next Olympics! It's a done deal. I just have to find a sport.*

After doing a little research on Olympic sports, Ruben decided he needed to pick a sport that would build on his strengths. He knew that he was a good athlete but not a great athlete. His strength was perseverance. He never quit anything. In fact, he had earned the nickname Bulldog in high school. He figured he had to find a sport so tough, a sport with so many broken bones, that there would be lots of quitters. That way maybe he could rise to the top on the attrition rate! He finally settled on the luge.

Next he wrote *Sports Illustrated* (this was before the Internet) and asked, "Where do you go to learn how to luge?" They wrote back, "Lake Placid, New York. That's where they had the Olympics in 1936 and 1980. That's where the track is." Ruben picked up the phone and called Lake Placid.

"I'm an athlete in Houston and I want to learn how to luge so I can be in the Olympics in four years. Will you help me?"

The guy who answered the phone asked, "How old are you?"

"Twenty-one years old."

"Twenty-one? You're way too old. You're ten years too late. We start them when they're ten years old. Forget it."

But Ruben couldn't forget it, and he started to tell the man his life story to buy some time until he thought of something. Along the way he happened to say that he was born in Argentina.

All of a sudden, the man on the other end of the phone got excited. "Argentina? Why didn't you say so? If you'll go for Argentina, we'll help you." It turns out the sport of luge was in danger of being dropped from the Olympics because there weren't enough countries competing on the international level. "If you'll go for Argentina and somehow we can get you into the top fifty ranked lugers in the world in four years, which is what you'll need to make it into the Olympics, it would add one more country to the sport of luge, and that would make it a stronger sport. If you make it, you'd be helping the U.S. team." Then he added, "Before you come all the way to Lake Placid, you have to know two things. Number one: if you want to do it at your age and you want to do it in only four years, it will be brutal. Nine out of every ten guys quit. Number two: expect to break some bones."

Ruben thought, *Great! This works right into my plan. I'm not a quitter. The harder it is, the easier it is for me.*

"I wondered why there was such a bad smell in here."

A few days later Ruben Gonzalez was walking down Main Street in Lake Placid looking for the U.S. Olympic Training Center. A day later, he was in a beginner's class with 14 other aspiring Olympians. The first day was miserable, and he even thought of quitting, but with the help of a friend he recommitted to his Olympic dream and, though all 14 of the other aspirants eventually quit before the end of the first season, Ruben finished the summer training.

Four grueling years later, Ruben Gonzalez realized his dream when he walked into the opening ceremonies of the 1988 Calgary Winter Olympics. He returned again in Albertville in 1992 and Salt Lake City for the 2000 Winter Games. Ruben Gonzalez, because he took immediate and persistent action on his dream, will always be a "three-time Olympian."

Successful People Have a Bias for Action

Most successful people I know have a low tolerance for excessive planning and talking about it. They are antsy to get going. They want to get started. They want the games to begin. A good example of this is my friend Bob Kriegel's son Otis. When Otis came home for the summer with his new girlfriend after his freshman year in college, they both began looking for jobs. While Otis just picked up the phone and started calling around to see who might need someone, his girlfriend spent the first week writing and rewriting her résumé. By the end of the second day, Otis had landed a job. His girlfriend was still rewriting her résumé. Otis just got into action. He figured if someone asked for a résumé, he'd deal with it then.

Planning has its place, but it must be kept in perspective. Some people spend their whole lives waiting for the perfect time to do something. There's rarely a "perfect" time to do anything. What is important is to just get started. Get into the game. Get on the playing field. Once you do, you will start to get feedback that will help you make the corrections you need to make to be successful. Once you are in action, you will start learning at a much more rapid rate.

Ready, Fire, Aim!

Most people are familiar with the phrase "Ready, aim, fire!" The problem is that too many people spend their whole life aiming and never firing. They are always getting ready, getting it perfect. The quickest way to hit a target is to fire, see where the bullet landed, and then adjust your aim accordingly. If the hit was 2 inches above the target, lower your aim a little. Fire again. See where it is now. Keep firing and keep readjusting. Soon you are hitting the bull's-eye. The same is true for anything.

When we started marketing the first *Chicken Soup for the Soul®* book, it occurred to me that it would be a good idea to give away free excerpts from the book to small and local newspapers in exchange for them printing a box at the end of the story telling people that the story was excerpted from *Chicken Soup for the Soul®*, which was available at their local bookstore or by calling our 800 number. I had never done this before, so I wasn't sure if there was a correct way to submit a story to a newspaper or magazine, so I just sent off a story from the book entitled "Remember, You Are Raising Children, Not Flowers!" that I had written about my neighbor and his son, along with a cover letter to the editor of *L.A. Parent* magazine. The letter read:

September 13, 1993

Jack Bierman
L.A. Parent

Dear Jack,

I would like to submit this article for publication in
L.A. Parent. I have enclosed a brief bio. I would like
you to print the little blurb I included on my new book
Chicken Soup for the Soul® with my article. If you
would like a copy of the book, I would be more than
happy to send one to you!

Thank you for your time.
Sincerely,

Jack Canfield

Encl: article "Remember, You Are Raising Children,
Not Flowers!"

A few weeks later, I received the following letter back:

Dear Jack:

I was annoyed by your fax. How dare you tell me to
include "the little blurb on your book." How could
you assume I'd be interested in this little bit of
unsolicited word processing. Then I read the article.
Needless to say, I'll run your little blurb and then
some!

I was moved by this exercise and am sure it will touch

the hearts of our 200,000 plus readers from here to San Diego.

Has it ever appeared anywhere in my demographic? If so, where? I look forward to working with you on raising children, not flowers.

Best regards,

Jack Bierman, Editor in Chief

I had not known how to submit a proper query letter to an editor. There was an accepted format that I was unaware of. But I took action anyway. In a subsequent phone call, Jack Bierman generously taught me the correct way to submit an article to a magazine. He gave me feedback on how to do it better next time. Now I was in the game and I was learning from my experience. Ready, fire, aim!

Within a month I had submitted that same article to over 50 local and regional parenting magazines all across the United States. Thirty-five of them published it, introducing *Chicken Soup for the Soul®* to over 6 million parents.

Quit Waiting

It's time to quit waiting for

Perfection
Inspiration
Permission

Reassurance
Someone to change
The right person to come along
The kids to leave home
A more favorable horoscope
The new administration to take over
An absence of risk
Someone to discover you
A clear set of instructions
More self-confidence
The pain to go away

Get on with it already!

Satisfaction Comes from Enough Action

Have you ever noticed that the last six letters in the word *satisfaction* are *a-c-t-i-o-n*? In Latin, the word *satis* means "enough." What the ancient Romans understood clearly was that enough action ultimately produces satisfaction.

Do It Now!

My mentor, W. Clement Stone, used to hand out lapel pins that said "Do it now." When you have an inspired impulse to take action, do it now. Ray Kroc, the founder of McDonald's, said, "There are three keys to success: 1. Being at the right place at the right time. 2. Knowing you are there. 3. Taking action."

On March 24, 1975, Chuck Wepner, a relatively unknown 30-to-1 underdog, did what no one thought he could do – he went 15 rounds with the world heavyweight champion Muhammad Ali. In the ninth round, he reached Ali's chin with a right hand, knocking the champion to the ground – shocking both Ali and the fans watching the fight. Wepner was only seconds away from being the world's heavyweight champion. However, Ali went on to win the 15-round bout and retain his title.

Over a thousand miles away, a struggling actor named Sylvester Stallone watched the fight on a newly purchased television set. Though Stallone had contemplated the idea of writing a screenplay about a down-and-out fighter getting a title shot before he saw the Ali–Wepner fight, he didn't think it was plausible. But after seeing Wepner, whom most people didn't know, fighting the most well-known fighter of all time, all he thought was *Get me a pencil*. He began to write that night, and 3 days later, he had completed the script for *Rocky*, which went on to win three Oscars, including one for best picture, thus launching Stallone's multimillion-dollar movie career.

Give Me a Break!

A story is told of a man who goes to church and prays, "God, I need a break. I need to win the state lottery. I'm counting on you, God." Having not won the lottery, the man returns to church a week later and once again prays, "God, about that state lottery … I've been kind to my wife. I've given up drinking. I've been really good. Give me a break. Let me win the lottery."

A week later, still no richer, he returns to pray once again. "God, I don't seem to be getting through to you on this state lottery thing. I've been using positive self-talk, saying affirmations, and visualizing the money. Give me a break, God. Let me win the lottery."

Suddenly the heavens open up, white light and heavenly music flood into the church, and a deep voice says, "My son, give me a break! Buy a lottery ticket!"

Fail Forward

No man ever became great or good except through many and great mistakes.

William E. Gladstone – Former prime minister of Great Britain

Many people fail to take action because they're afraid to fail. Successful people, on the other hand, realize that failure is an important part of the learning process. They know that failure is just a way we learn by trial and error. Not only do we need to stop being so afraid of failure but we also need to be willing to fail – even eager to fail. I call this kind of instructive failure "failing forward." Simply get started, make mistakes, listen to the feedback, correct, and keep moving forward toward the goal. Every experience will yield up more useful information that you can apply the next time.

This principle is perhaps demonstrated most compellingly in the area of start-up businesses. For instance, venture capitalists know that most businesses fail. But in the venture capital industry, a new statistic is emerging. If the founding entrepreneur is 55 years or older, the business has a 73% better chance of survival. These older entrepreneurs have already learned from their mistakes. They're simply a better risk because through a lifetime of learning from their failures, they have developed a knowledge base, a skill set, and a self-confidence that better enables them to move through the obstacles to success.

Frank and Ernest

EMPLOYMENT

I DON'T HAVE ANY FORMAL EDUCATION, SO I BROUGHT YOU A LIST OF THE MISTAKES I'VE LEARNED FROM.

©1990 Thaves. Reprinted with permission. Newspaper dist. by NEA, Inc.

You can never learn less; you can only learn more. The reason I know so much is because I have made so many mistakes.

Buckminster Fuller – Mathematician and philosopher who never graduated from college but received 46 honorary doctorates

One of my favorite stories is about a famous research scientist who had made several very important medical breakthroughs. He was being interviewed by a newspaper reporter, who asked him why he thought he was able to achieve so much more than the average person. In other words, what set him so far apart from others?

He responded that it all came from a lesson his mother had taught him when he was 2 years old. He'd been trying to take a bottle of milk out of the refrigerator, when he lost his grip and spilled the entire contents on the kitchen floor. His mother, instead of scolding him, said, "What a wonderful mess you've made! I've rarely seen such a huge puddle of milk. Well, the damage is already done. Would you like to get down and play in the milk before we clean it up?"

Indeed, he did. And, after a few minutes, his mother continued, "You know, whenever you make a mess like this, eventually you have to clean it up. So, how would you like to do that? We could use a towel, sponge, or mop. Which do you prefer?"

After they were finished cleaning up the milk, she said, "What we have here is a failed experiment in how to carry a big bottle of milk with two tiny hands. Let's go out in the backyard, fill the bottle with water, and see if you can discover a way to carry it without dropping it." And they did.

What a wonderful lesson!

The scientist then remarked that it was at that moment that he knew he didn't have to be afraid to make mistakes. Instead, he learned that *mistakes are just opportunities for learning something new* – which, after all, is what scientific experiments are all about.

That bottle of spilled milk led to a lifetime of learning experiences – experiences that were the building blocks of a lifetime of world-renowned successes and medical breakthroughs!

Principle 14

Feel the Fear
and Do It Anyway

We come this way but once. We can either tiptoe
through life and hope that we get to death without
being too badly bruised or we can live a full, complete
life achieving our goals and realizing our wildest dreams.

Bob Proctor – Self-made millionaire, radio and
TV personality, and success trainer

I have insecurities. But whatever I'm insecure about, I
don't dissect it, but I'll go after it and say, "What am I
afraid of?" I bet the average successful person can tell
you they've failed so much more than they've had
success. I've had far more failures than I've had
successes. With every commercial I've gotten, there
were 200 I didn't get. You have to go after what you're
afraid of.

Kevin Sorbo – Actor who starred in the television series
Hercules: The Legendary Journeys

As you move forward on your journey from where you are
to where you want to be, you are going to have to confront your fears. Fear is natural. Whenever you start a new
project, take on a new venture, or put yourself out there,

there is usually fear. Unfortunately, most people let fear stop them from taking the necessary steps to achieve their dreams. Successful people, on the other hand, feel the fear along with the rest of us but don't let it keep them from doing anything they want to do – *or have to do*. They understand that fear is something to be acknowledged, experienced, and taken along for the ride. They have learned, as author Susan Jeffers suggests, to feel the fear and do it anyway.

Why Are We So Fearful?

Millions of years ago, fear was our body's way of signaling us that we were out of our comfort zone. It alerted us to possible danger, and gave us the burst of adrenaline we needed to run away. Unfortunately, though this response was useful in the days when saber-toothed tigers were chasing us, today most of our threats are not all that life-threatening.

Today, fear is more of a signal that we must stay alert and cautious. We can feel fear, but we can still move forward anyway. Think of your fear as a 2-year-old child who doesn't want to go grocery shopping with you. You wouldn't let a 2-year-old's mentality run your life. Because you must buy groceries, you'll just have to take the 2-year-old along with you. Fear is no different. In other words, acknowledge that fear exists but don't let it keep you from doing important tasks.

You Have to Be Willing to Feel the Fear

Some people will do anything to avoid the uncomfortable feeling of fear. If you are one of those people, you run an even bigger risk of never getting what you want in life. Most of the good stuff requires taking a risk. And the nature of a risk is that it doesn't always work out. People do lose their investments, people do forget their lines, people do fall off mountains, people do die in accidents. But as the old adage so wisely tells us, "Nothing ventured, nothing gained."

When I interviewed Jeff Arch, who wrote the screenplay for the movie *Sleepless in Seattle*, he told me:

I am about to launch the biggest gamble of my life – writing and directing a two-million-dollar comedy, when I have never directed before, and using my own money plus raising other money to fund it – and I really need to succeed at this. Really, it's an all-or-nothing situation. And the thing that I'm experiencing right now, which I think is really important and that a lot of people who write about success leave out, is you've got to be willing to be terrified. Because I am terrified about what I'm about to do. But it's not immobilizing. It's a good terrified; it's a terrified that keeps you on your toes.

I know I have to do this because I had a very clear vision, and I am willing to stand alone without agreement from the industry, which I learned you have to do from when I was pitching *Sleepless in Seattle*. Believe me, when you start pitching an idea about a love story where the lead characters don't meet, you are alone. Everybody told me, "You're out of your freaking mind." And one thing I discovered is when everyone says you're out of your mind, you just might be on to something. So, I had these reference points from my past experience. I was alone back then. And I was right. I've learned you have to believe in your dream. Because even if everyone is telling you you're wrong, that still might not mean anything – you just might be right.

You reach a point where you say, "This is it. I'm throwing everything into this. And it's got to succeed." It's like the Spanish conquistador Hernando Cortez in 1519. To prevent any thought of retreating from his mission, after he landed in Mexico, he burned all of his ships. Well, I've rented new ships just for the sake of burning them. I took out loans on ships that weren't even mine. I'm throwing money, credibility – every single thing there is – into my new project. And it's either going to be a home run or a strikeout – not a single or a double.

I know there's a terror in doing this, but there's also this confidence. It isn't going to kill me. It might make me broke, it might leave me in debt, it might make me lose credibility, and it might make the journey back a whole lot harder. But unlike Cortez, I'm not in a business where they kill you if you goof up. I think one of the secrets to my success is that I'm willing to be terrified, and I think a lot of people are not willing to be scared to death. And that's why they don't achieve the big dream.

Fantasized Experiences Appearing Real

Another important aspect to remember about fear is that, as humans, we've also evolved to the stage where almost all of our fears are now self-created. We frighten ourselves by fantasizing negative outcomes to any activity we might pursue or experience. Luckily, because we are the ones doing the fantasizing, we are also the ones who can stop the fear and bring ourselves into a state of clarity and peace by facing the actual facts, rather than giving in to our imaginations. We can choose to be sensible. Psychologists like to say that fear means

Fantasized
Experiences
Appearing
Real

To help you better understand how we actually bring un-founded fear into our lives, make a list of the things you are afraid to *do*. This is not a list of things you are afraid *of*, such as being afraid *of* spiders, but things you're afraid to *do*, such as being afraid to pick up a spider. For example, I am afraid to

- Ask my boss for a raise
- Ask Sally out for a date
- Go skydiving
- Leave my kids home alone with a sitter
- Leave this job that I hate
- Take 2 weeks away from the office
- Ask my friends to look at my new business opportunity
- Delegate any part of my job to others

Now go back and restate each fear using the following format:

I want to ...., and I scare myself by imagining

....

The key words are *I scare myself by imagining*. All fear is self-created by imagining some negative outcome in the future. Using some of the same fears listed above, the new format would look like this:

- I want to ask my boss for a raise, and I scare myself by imagining he would say no and be angry with me for asking.

- I want to ask Sally out for a date, and I scare myself by imagining that she would say no and I would feel embarrassed.
- I want to go skydiving, and I scare myself by imagining that my parachute wouldn't open and I would be killed.
- I want to leave my kids home with a sitter, and I scare myself by imagining that something terrible would happen to them.
- I want to leave this job I hate to pursue my dream, and I scare myself by imagining I would go bankrupt and lose my house.
- I want to ask my friends to look at my new business opportunity, and I scare myself by imagining they will think I am only interested in making money off of them.

Can you see that you are the one creating the fear?

How to Get Rid of Fear

I have lived a long life and had many troubles, most of which never happened.

Mark Twain – Celebrated American author and humorist

One way to actually *disappear* your fear is to ask yourself what you're imagining that is scary to you, and then replace that image with its positive opposite.

When I was flying to Orlando recently to give a talk, I noticed the woman next to me was gripping the arms of her seat so tightly her knuckles were turning white. I introduced myself, told her I was a trainer, and said I couldn't help but notice her hands. I asked her, "Are you afraid?"

"Yes."

"Would you be willing to close your eyes and tell me what thoughts or images you are experiencing in your head?"

After she closed her eyes, she replied, "I just keep imagining the plane not getting off the runway and crashing."

"I see. Tell me, what are you headed to Orlando for?"

"I'm going there to spend four days with my grandchildren at Disney World."

"Great. What's your favorite ride at Disney World?"

"It's a Small World."

"Wonderful. Can you imagine being at Disney World in one of the gondolas with your grandchildren in the It's a Small World attraction?"

"Yes."

"Can you see the smiles and the looks of wonder on your grandchildren's faces as they watch all the little puppets and figures from the different countries bobbing up and down and spinning around?"

"Uh-huh."

At that point I started to sing, "It's a small world after all; it's a small world after all ..."

Her face relaxed, her breathing deepened, and her hands released their grip on the arms of the seat.

In her mind, she was already at Disney World. She had replaced the catastrophic picture of the plane crashing with a positive image of her desired outcome, and instantly her fear disappeared.[1]

You can use this same technique to disappear any fear that you might ever experience.

Replace the Physical Sensations Fear Brings

Another technique that works for relieving fear is to focus on the *physical sensations* you're currently feeling – sensations you're probably just identifying as fear. Next, focus on those feelings you would *like* to be experiencing instead – courage, self-confidence, calm, joy.

Fix these two different impressions firmly in your mind's eye, then slowly shuttle back and forth between the two, spending about 15 seconds in each one. After a minute or two, the fear will dissipate and you will find yourself in a neutral, centered place.

Remember When You Triumphed in the Face of Fear

Did you ever learn to dive off a diving board? If so, you probably remember the first time you walked to the edge of the board and looked down. The water looked a lot deeper than it really was. And considering the height of the board and the height of your eyes above the board, it probably looked like a *very* long way down.

You were scared. But did you look at your mom or dad or the diving instructor and say, "You know, I'm just too afraid to do this right now. I think I'll go do some therapy on this, and if I can get rid of my fear, I'll come back and try again …"?

No! You didn't say that.

You felt the fear, somehow mustered up courage from somewhere, and jumped into the water. You felt the fear and did it anyway.

When you surfaced, you probably swam like crazy to the side of the pool and took a few well-earned deep breaths. Somewhere, there was a little rush of adrenaline, the thrill of having survived a risk, plus the thrill of jumping through the air into the water. After a minute, you probably did it again, and then again and again – enough to where it got to be really fun. Pretty soon, all of the fear was gone and you were doing cannonballs to splash your friends and maybe even learning how to do a backflip.

If you can remember that experience or the first time

you drove a car or the first time you kissed someone on a date, you've got the model for everything that happens in life. New experiences will always feel a little scary. They're supposed to. That's the way it works. But every time you face a fear and do it anyway, you build up that much more confidence in your abilities.

Scale Down the Risk

Anthony Robbins says, "If you can't, you must, and if you must, you can." I agree. It is those very things that we are most afraid to do that provide the greatest liberation and growth for us.

If a fear is so big that it paralyzes you, scale down the amount of risk. Take on smaller challenges and work your way up. If you're starting your first job in sales, call on prospects or customers you think will be the easiest to sell to first. If you're asking for money for your business, practice on those lending sources whom you wouldn't want to get a loan from anyway. If you're anxious about taking on new responsibilities at work, start by asking to do parts of a project you're interested in. If you're learning a new sport, start at lower levels of skill. Master those skills you need to learn, move through your fears, and then take on bigger challenges.

When Your Fear Is Really a Phobia

Some fears are so strong that they can actually immobilize you. If you have a full-blown phobia, such as fear of flying or fear of being in an elevator, it can seriously inhibit your ability to be successful. Fortunately there is a simple solution for most phobias. The Five-Minute Phobia Cure, developed by Dr. Roger Callahan, is easy to learn and can be self-administered as well as facilitated by a professional.

I learned about this magical technique from Dr. Callahan's book and video and have used it successfully in my seminars for more than 15 years. The process uses a simple but precise pattern of tapping on various points of the body while you simultaneously imagine the object or experience that stimulates your phobic reaction. It acts in much the same way as a virus in a computer program by permanently interrupting the "program" or sequence of events that occur in the brain between the initial sighting of the thing you are afraid of (such as seeing a snake or stepping into an airplane) and the physical response (such as sweating, shaking, shallow breathing, or weak knees) you experience.

When I was leading a seminar for real estate agents, a woman revealed that she had a phobia about walking up stairs. In fact, she had experienced it that very morning, when in response to her request for directions to the seminar, the bellman had pointed to a huge staircase leading to the grand ballroom. Fortunately, there was also an elevator, so she made it to the seminar. If there hadn't been, she would have turned around and driven home. She admitted that she had never been on the second floor of any home she had ever sold. She would pretend she had already been up there, tell the prospective buyers what they would find on the second floor, on the basis of her reading of the listing sheet, and then let them explore it on their own.

I did the Five-Minute Phobia Cure with her and then took all 100 people out to the same hotel stairway that had petrified her earlier in the day. With no hesitation, heavy breathing, or drama, she walked up and down the stairs twice. It is that simple.[2]

Take a leap!

> Come to the edge, He said.
> They said: We are afraid.
> Come to the edge, He said.
> They came. He pushed them,
> And they flew …
>
> **Guillaume Apollinaire** – Avant-garde French poet

All the successful people I know have been willing to take a chance – a leap of faith – even though they were afraid. Sometimes they were terrified, but they knew if they didn't act, the opportunity would pass them by. They trusted their intuition and they simply went for it.

> Progress always involves risk; you can't steal second base and keep your foot on first.
> **Frederick Wilcox**

Mike Kelley lives in paradise and owns several companies under the umbrella of Beach Activities of Maui. With only a year of college under his belt (he never did return to get his degree), Mike left Las Vegas at age 19 for the islands of Hawaii and ended up selling suntan lotion by the pool at a hotel in Maui. From these humble beginnings, Mike went on to create a company with 175 employees and over $5 million in annual revenues that provides recreational experiences (catamaran and scuba diving excursions) for tourists and concierge services and business centers for many of the island's hotels.

Mike credits much of his success to always being willing to take a leap when needed. When Beach Activities of Maui was attempting to expand its business, there was an important hotel whose business he wanted, but a competitor had held the contract for over 15 years. To maintain a competitive edge, Mike always reads the trade journals and keeps an ear open to what is happening in his business. One day he read that this hotel was changing general managers, and the new general manager who would be coming in lived in Copper Mountain, Colorado. This got

Mike to thinking: Because it is so hard to get through all of the gatekeepers to secure a meeting with a general manager, maybe he should try to contact him before he actually moved to Hawaii. Mike wrestled with what would be the best way to contact him. Should he write a letter? Should he call him on the phone? As he pondered these options, his friend Doug suggested, "Why don't you just hop on a plane and go see him?"

Always one to take action and take it now, Mike quickly put together a pro forma and a proposal and hopped on a plane the next night. After flying all night, he arrived in Colorado, rented a car and drove the 2 hours out to Copper Mountain, and showed up unannounced at the new general manager's office. He explained who he was, congratulated him on his new promotion, told him that he looked forward to having him in Maui, and asked for a few moments to tell him about his company and what it could do for his hotel.

Mike didn't get the contract during that first meeting, but the fact that a young kid was so confident in himself and his services that he would take a leap of faith to jump on a plane and fly all the way to Denver and drive out into the middle of Colorado on the off chance that he would be able to get together with him left such a huge impression on the general manager that when he did finally get to Hawaii, Mike secured the contract, which, over the ensuing 15 years, has been worth hundreds of thousands of dollars to Mike's bottom line.

Taking a Leap Can Transform Your Life

Authority is 20% given and 80% taken … so take it!

Peter Ueberroth – Organizer of the 1984 Summer Olympics and commissioner of Major League Baseball, 1984–1988

Multimillionaire Dr. John Demartini is a resounding success by anyone's standards. He's married to a beautiful and brilliant woman – Athena Starwoman, the world-famous astrologer who consults and writes for 24 well-known magazines, including *Vogue*. Together, they own several homes in Australia. And they spend over 60 days a year together circumnavigating the globe in their $3 million luxury apartment onboard the $550 million ocean liner *World of ResidenSea* – a residence they purchased after selling their Trump Tower apartment in New York City.

The author of 54 training programs and 13 books, John spends the year traveling the world speaking and conducting his courses on financial success and life mastery.

But John didn't start out rich and successful. At age 7, he was found to have a learning disability and was told that he would never read, write, or communicate normally. At 14, he dropped out of school, left his Texas home, and headed for the California coast. By 17, he had ended up in Hawaii, surfing the waves of Oahu's famed North Shore, where he almost died from strychnine poisoning. His road to recovery led him to Dr. Paul Bragg, a 93-year-old man who changed John's life by giving him one simple affirmation to repeat: "I am a genius and I apply my wisdom."

Inspired by Dr. Bragg, John went to college, earned his bachelor's degree from the University of Houston and later his doctoral degree from the Texas College of Chiropractic.

When he opened his first chiropractic office in Houston, John started with just 970 square feet of space. Within 9 months, he'd more than doubled that and was offering free classes on healthy living. When attendance grew, John was ready to expand again. It was then he took a leap that changed his career forever.

"It was Monday," John said. "The shoe store next door had vacated over the weekend." *What a perfect lecture hall*, John thought as he quickly phoned the leasing company.

When no one called him back, John concluded they weren't going to rent the space soon, so he took a leap.

"I called a locksmith to come out and open up the place," John said. "I thought the worst thing they would do was charge me rent."

He quickly transformed the space into a lecture hall and within days was holding free talks there on a nightly basis. Because the space was located right next to a movie theater, he added a loudspeaker so moviegoers could hear his lectures as they walked to their cars. Hundreds began attending classes and eventually became patients.

John's practice grew rapidly. Yet nearly 6 months went by before the property manager came to investigate.

"You've got a lot of courage," the manager said. "You remind me of me." In fact, he was so impressed with

John's daring, he even gave John 6 months' free rent! "Anybody that has the courage to do what you did deserves it," he told him. The manager later invited John down to his office, where he offered him a quarter of a million dollars a year to come work for him. John turned it down because he had other plans, but it was a huge validation of his courage to act.

Taking a leap helped John build a thriving practice, which he later sold to begin consulting full time with other chiropractors.

"Taking that leap opened up a doorway for me," John said. "If I'd held back … if I had been cautious … I wouldn't have made the breakthrough that gave me the life I live today."

Oh, What the Heck – Just Go for It!

Do you want to be safe and good, or do you want to take a chance and be great?

Jimmy Johnson – Coach who led the Dallas Cowboys football team to two consecutive Super Bowl championships in 1992 and 1993

Living at risk is jumping off the cliff and building your wings on the way down.

Ray Bradbury – Author of more than 500 literary works

When Richard Paul Evans wrote his first book, *The Christmas Box*, it was simply a gift of love to his two young daughters. Later, he made photocopies for family and friends, and word spread quickly about this heartwarming tale. Spurred on by this positive reaction, Rick sought a publisher for the book. When there were no takers, Rick decided to publish it himself.

To promote the book, he took a booth at a regional American Booksellers Association conference, where, among other activities, celebrity authors were signing books at one end of the exhibit hall. Rick noticed these celebrity authors were the only ones getting attention from the press. He also noticed that when the next group of celebrities arrived for their scheduled time, one author had failed to arrive.

With his fear being crowded out by his courage and commitment to his dream, Rick decided to take a leap. He picked up two boxes of books, walked toward the empty chair, sat down, and began to sign.

Seeing him at the table, a woman from the show approached him to ask him to leave. Undaunted, Evans looked up and before she could speak said, "Sorry I'm late." The stunned woman just looked at him and asked, "Can I get you something to drink?" The next year, Evans was the premier author at the show as his book climbed to number 1 on the *New York Times* Best-Seller List. Since then, *The Christmas Box* has sold more than 8 million copies in 18 languages and has been made into an Emmy Award-winning CBS television movie. The book, which had been previously

rejected by several major publishing houses, was eventually purchased by Simon & Schuster for a record $4.2 million.

Be Willing to Put It All on the Line for Your Dream

Only those who dare to fail greatly
can ever achieve greatly.

Robert F. Kennedy – Former attorney general and U.S. senator

In January of 1981, real estate investor Robert Allen took
a challenge – putting it all on the line – that would make
or break his new career as an author and seminar leader.
He was looking for ways to promote his new book *Nothing Down: How to Buy Real Estate with Little or No Money
Down*. Frustrated with the ad his publisher's public relations department had created, Bob found himself spout-
ing off the top of his head what he felt needed to be said
in the ad. "We need to demonstrate that someone can buy
property with nothing down."

His publisher responded, "What do you mean?"

Bob said, "I don't know. You could take me to a city,
take away my wallet and give me a hundred bucks, and I'd
buy a property."

"How long would it take you?"

"I don't know, maybe a week, maybe three or four days
– seventy-two hours."

"Can you do that?"

Bob found himself looking at the abyss, realizing he'd never done that before and not knowing for sure if he could do it now. His head was saying no and his heart was saying yes.

Bob went with his heart and said, "Yeah, I probably can do that."

"Well, if you can do that, that's the title of the ad we're going to run: 'So then he said he'd take away my wallet, give me a hundred-dollar bill, and send me out to buy a piece of real estate using none of my own money.' "

Bob said, "Okay, let it rip," and they ran the ad, which was very successful. Within a few months after being released, the book was number one on the *Time* magazine best seller list and it ended up being on the *New York Times* Best-Seller List for 46 weeks.

Later that year Bob got a call from a reporter at the *Los Angeles Times* who said, "We don't think you can do what you say you can do."

Bob replied, "Well, I'd be glad to be challenged," and then quipped, "How about a date sometime in 2050?" But the *Times* was serious – serious about taking Bob down. The reporter said, "I am going to take you down. We don't like your ad. We think you're a fraud, and you're going down." Scared, but determined he had to take the challenge, Bob set it up for 4 weeks later.

On January 12, 1981, the reporter from the *Times* met him at the Marriott Hotel just east of Los Angeles International Airport. Bob hadn't slept much the night before. In fact, he hadn't slept much for the entire month before. He lay awake at night wondering if he could really pull it off in such a short time. Taking the challenge had felt like the right thing to do, but he still didn't know if he could do it.

Together they boarded a plane and flew to San Francisco, and Bob hit the ground running. He immediately went to a real estate office and started writing no-money-down offers, and they promptly escorted them out of the office, which Bob recalls "was not a good way to start."

Bob started thinking, *Uh-oh, I'm in deep trouble now. I'm going to lose it all. It's gone. I'm not going to be able to pull this off. What was I thinking?* Was he scared? "Oh yeah, I was terrified." But he just made call after call after call and finally, toward the end of the first day, he started running into some success and found a property that somebody was willing to sell him. By the next morning, he had a signed offer.

So it had been just a little over 24 hours and he had bought his first property. Then Bob said, "We're not done yet. You gave me 72 hours. I've scheduled my life for this for the next 3 days. Let's see how many we can do." At this point, the reporter became his cheerleader. After all, the reporter had already lost the challenge, and the bigger he lost, the better the story.

Before, he was saying, "I'm going to take you down." Now it was, "Hey, Bob, go for it, boy. If you're going to beat me, beat me bad." And Bob did. He bought seven properties worth $700,000 in 57 hours and gave the reporter $20 back out of the $100 he had started with.

The subsequent article, which was syndicated by the *Los Angeles Times* and picked up by dozens of newspapers across the country, launched Bob's career. He had risked it all, and he had won big time! His book *Nothing Down* went on to sell over a million copies and became the eleventh best-selling hardcover book of the 1980s.[3]

The Challenge

If you want to achieve a high goal, you're going to have to take some chances.

Alberto Salazar – Winner of three consecutive New York City Marathons in 1980, 1981, and 1982, and now a spokesperson for Nike

Robert Allen's life seems to have been built on leaping into the void to prove that his methods can and do work – for everyone, no matter their status – to produce wealth and abundance in their lives. Even after his stunning success of buying seven houses in 72 hours with no money down in San Francisco, the press still hounded him with, "Well, sure, *you* can do it, but the average person couldn't do it." Bob's message was that *anybody* could buy property with no money down, but the press kept countering with "Well, you're not just anybody."

Bob told me, "I became so infuriated with the press that I said, 'You can send me to any unemployment line' – and I remember stuff just coming out of my mouth, not knowing where it was coming from – 'let me select someone who's broke, out of work, and discouraged, and in two days time I'll teach him the secrets of wealth. And in ninety days he'll be back on his feet with five thousand dollars cash in the bank, and he'll never set foot in an unemployment line again.' "

Bob went to St. Louis, asked the ex-mayor to oversee the project, went to the unemployment office, and handed out 1,200 flyers offering to teach people how to become financially independent. Expecting the room to be filled to the rafters, he had the room set up for 300 chairs, but only 50 people showed up – and half those people left at the first break as soon as they heard how much work was going to be involved. After an extensive interview process, only three couples remained. He worked with those three couples. Though all of them did deals in the first 90 days, technically only one of them made the $5,000 cash in the 3-month period. All of them did more deals that year and changed their lives in a variety of different ways. The couple that made the $5,000 cash in the first 90 days also went on to make over $100,000 in the next 12 months. Once again, by taking a huge risk, by leaping into the void, Bob had proved his point and finally made the press back off.

He went on to write a book about the experience called *The Challenge.*[4] While it was his least successful book, selling only 65,000 copies, it became his most profitable because it was the first book he ever put his name, address, and phone numbers in. Over 4,000 of the people who read that book called Bob's office and eventually paid

$5,000 to attend Bob's ongoing training program. That's $20 million – not bad for being willing to pay the price of putting his butt on the line one more time.

> The secret to my success is that I bit off more than I could chew and chewed as fast as I could.
>
> **Paul Hogan** – Actor who portrayed Crocodile Dundee

High Intention ... Low Attachment

If you want to remain calm and peaceful as you go through life, you have to have high intention and low attachment. You do everything you can to create your desired outcomes, and then you let it go. Sometimes you don't get the intended result by the date that you want. That is life. You just keep moving in the direction of your goal until you get there. Sometimes the universe has other plans, and often they are better than the ones you had in mind. That is why I recommend adding the phrase "this or something better" to the end of your affirmations.

When I was vacationing with my family on a cruise in Tahiti two summers ago, my son Christopher and my stepson Travis, both 12 at the time, and I set out on a guided bicycle tour around the island of Bora-Bora with some other members from our cruise ship. My intention for the day was a bonding experience with my two sons. The wind was blowing really hard that day and the trip was a difficult one. At one point, Stevie Eller, who was struggling along with her 11-year-old grandson, took a nasty fall and badly cut her leg. Because there were only a few others in the back of the pack with us, we stayed behind to help her. There were no homes or stores and virtually no traffic on the far side of the island, meaning that there was no way to call for help, so after attempting some crude first aid, we decided to all push on together. Bored with the slow pace, my boys took off ahead, and I spent the next several hours pedaling and walking next to my new friend until we eventually reached a hotel where she called for a taxi and I rejoined my sons, who had stopped for a swim, for the rest of the trip around the island. That night Stevie and her husband, Karl, asked us to join their family for dinner.

It turned out that they were on the nominating committee for the 2004 International Achievement Summit sponsored by the Academy of Achievement, whose mission was to "inspire youth with new dreams of achievement in a world of boundless opportunity" by bringing together over 200 university and graduate student delegates from around the world to interact with contemporary leaders who have achieved the difficult or impossible in service to their fellow humans. After our time together, they decided to nominate me to become a member of the academy and receive their Golden Plate Award, joining previous recipients such as former president Bill Clinton,

Placido Domingo, George Lucas, New York mayor Rudolph Giuliani, U.S. senator John McCain, former prime minister of Israel Shimon Peres, and Archbishop Desmond Tutu. Because my nomination was accepted, I was able to attend the annual 4-day event with some of the brightest young future leaders and some of the most interesting and accomplished people in the world in 2004 and will be able to attend every year for the rest of my life – and I can even bring my sons to a future meeting!

Had I been totally attached to my original outcome of a day with my two sons and left Stevie to the care of others, I would have missed an even bigger opportunity that spontaneously came my way. I have learned over the years that whenever one door seemingly closes, another door opens. You just have to keep positive, stay aware, and look to see what it is. Instead of getting upset when things don't unfold as you anticipated, always ask yourself the question "What's the possibility that this is?"

Principle 15

Ask! Ask! Ask!

You've got to ask. Asking is, in my opinion,
the world's most powerful and neglected
secret to success and happiness.

Percy Ross – Self-made multimillionaire and philanthropist

History is filled with examples of incredible riches and astounding benefits people have received simply by asking
for them. Yet surprisingly, asking – one of the most powerful success principles of all – is still a challenge that
holds most people back. If you are not afraid to ask anybody for anything, then skip over this chapter. But if you
are like most people, you may be holding yourself back
by not asking for the information, assistance, support,
money, and time that you need to fulfill your vision and
make your dreams come true.

Why People Are Afraid to Ask

Why are people so afraid to ask? They are afraid of many
things such as looking needy, looking foolish, and looking stupid. But mostly they're afraid of experiencing rejection. They are afraid of hearing the word *no*.

The sad thing is that they're actually rejecting themselves in advance. They're saying no to themselves before anyone else even has a chance to.

When I was a graduate student at the school of education at the University of Chicago, I participated in a self-development group with 20 other people. During one of the exercises, one of the men asked one of the women if she found him attractive. I was both shocked by the boldness of the question and embarrassed for the asker – fearing what he might get as a response. As it turned out, she said that she did. Emboldened by his success, I then asked her if she found *me* attractive. After this little exercise in "bold asking," several of the women told us that they found it unbelievable how scared men were when it came to asking women for a date. She said, "You reject yourself before you even give us a chance to. Take the risk. We might say yes."

Don't assume that you are going to get a no. Take the risk to ask for whatever you need and want. If they say no, you are no worse off than when you started. If they say yes, you are a lot better off. Just by being willing to ask, you can get a raise, a donation, a room with an ocean view, a discount, a free sample, a date, a better assignment, the order, a more convenient delivery date, an extension, time off, or help with the housework.

How to Ask for What You Want

There's a specific science to asking for and getting what you want or need in life, and Mark Victor Hansen and I have written a whole book about it. And though I recommend you learn more by reading our book *The Aladdin Factor*, here are some quick tips to get you started:

1. **Ask as if you expect to get it.** Ask with a positive expectation. Ask from the place that you have already been given it. It's a done deal. Ask as if you expect to get a yes.

2. **Assume you can.** Don't start with the assumption that you can't get it. If you are going to assume, assume you *can* get an upgrade. Assume you *can* get a table by the window. Assume that you *can* return it without a sales slip. Assume that you *can* get a scholarship, that you *can* get a raise, that you *can* get tickets at this late date. Don't ever assume against yourself.

3. **Ask someone who can give it to you.** Qualify the person. "Who would I have to speak to to get …" "Who is authorized to make a decision about …" "What would have to happen for me to get …"

4. **Be clear and specific.** In my seminars, I often ask, "Who wants more money?" I pick someone who raises a hand, and I give that person a dollar. I say, "You now have more money. Are you satisfied?"

   The person usually says, "No, I want more than that."

   So I give the person a couple of quarters, and ask, "Is that enough for you?"

"No, I want more than that."

"Well, just how much do you want? We could play this game of 'more' for days and never get to what you want."

The person usually gives me a specific number, and then I point out how important it is to be specific. Vague requests produce vague results. Your requests need to be specific. When it comes to money, you need to ask for a specific amount.

Don't say: I want a raise.
Do say: I want a raise of $500 a month.

When it comes to when you want something done, don't say "soon" or "whenever it's convenient." Give a specific date and time.

Don't say: I want to spend some time with you this weekend.
Do say: I would like to go out for dinner and a movie with you on Sa*urday night. Would that work for you?

When it comes to a behavioral request, be specific. Say exactly what you want the person to do.

Don't say: I want more help around the house.
Do say: I want you to wash the dishes every night after dinner and take out the garbage Monday, Wednesday, and Friday nights.

5. **Ask repeatedly.** One of the most important principles of success is persistence, not giving up. Whenever you're asking others to participate in the fulfillment of your

goals, some people are going to say no. They may have other priorities, commitments, and reasons not to participate. It's not a reflection on you.

Just get used to the idea that there's going to be a lot of rejection along the way to the brass ring. The key is not to give up. When someone says no, you keep on asking. Why? Because when you keep on asking – even the same person again and again – you might get a yes …

On a different day
When the person is in a better mood
When you have new data to present
After you've proven your commitment to them
When circumstances have changed
When you've learned how to close better
When you've established better rapport
When the person trusts you more
When you have paid your dues
When the economy is better

Kids understand this success principle perhaps better than anyone. They will ask the same person for the same thing over and over again without any hesitation. They eventually wear you down.

I once read a story in *People* magazine about a man who asked the same woman more than 30 times to marry him. No matter how many times she said no, he kept coming back – and eventually she said yes!

A Telling Statistic

Herbert True, a marketing specialist at Notre Dame University, found that

- 44% of all salespeople quit trying after the first call
- 24% quit after the second call
- 14% quit after the third call
- 12% quit trying to sell their prospect after the fourth call

This means that 94% of all salespeople quit after the fourth call. But 60% of all sales are made after the fourth call. This revealing statistic shows that 94% of all salespeople don't give themselves a chance at 60% of the prospective buyers.

You may have the capacity, but you also have to have the tenacity! To be successful, you have to ask, ask, ask, ask, ask!

Ask, and It Shall Be Given to You

In 2000, Sylvia Collins flew all the way from Australia to Santa Barbara to take one of my weeklong seminars, where she learned about the power of asking. A year later, I received this letter from her.

I have taken a detour in my career path, and I'm selling new developments on the Gold Coast with a company called Gold Coast Property. I work with a team of guys mostly in their twenties! The skills I have acquired through your seminars have helped me to perform and be an active part of a winning team! I must tell you how having self-esteem and not being afraid to ask has impacted this office!

At a recent staff meeting, we were asked what we would like to do for our once-a-month team-building day. I asked Michael, the managing director, "What target would we have to reach for you to take us to an island for a week?"

Everyone around the table just went silent and looked at me; obviously it was out of everyone's comfort zone to ask such a thing. Michael looked around and then looked at me and said, "Well, if you reach … (and then he set a financial target), I'll take the whole team (ten of us) to the *Great Barrier Reef!"*

Well, the next month we reached the target and off we went to Lady Elliott Island for four days – airfares, accommodations, food, and activities all paid for by the company. We had the most amazing four days – we snorkeled together, had bonfires on the beach, played tricks on each other, and had so much fun!

Afterwards, Michael gave us another target and said he would take us to Fiji if we reached it, and we reached that target in December! Even though the company is paying for these trips, Michael is miles ahead from the enormous level of increased sales!

You Have Nothing to Lose and Everything to Gain by Asking

To be successful, you have to take risks, and one of the risks is the willingness to risk rejection. Here's an e-mail I received from Donna Hutcherson, who heard me speak at her company's convention in Scottsdale, Arizona.

> My husband Dale and I heard you at the Walsworth convention in early January; … Dale came as one of the spouses. … He was particularly impressed by your mention of not having anything to lose by asking or trying. After hearing you speak, he decided to go for one of his lifetime goals (and heart's desire) – a head football coaching position. He applied for four openings within my sales territory and Sebring High School called him back the next day, encouraging him to fill out the application online. He did so right away and could hardly sleep that night. After two interviews he was chosen over 61 other applicants. Today Dale accepted the position as head football coach at Sebring High School in Sebring, Florida.
>
> Thank you for your vision and inspiration.

Here is an excerpt from another e-mail I received from Donna this past summer:

Taking over a program that had back-to-back seasons with 1 win and 9 losses (and a reputation for giving up), Dale led the team to a winning record (with 4 "come-from-behind" wins in the last three minutes), a county championship, and only the 3rd playoff in the 78-year history of the school. He was also named County Coach of the Year and Sports Story of the Year. Most important is that he changed the lives of the many players, staff, and students with whom he worked.

Will You Give Me Some Money?

In 1997, 21-year-old Chad Pregracke set out on a one-man mission to clean up the Mississippi River. He started with a 20-foot boat and his own two hands. Since that time, he's cleared more than 1,000 miles of the Mississippi and another 435 miles of the Illinois River, pulling more than 1 million tons of debris from the riverbanks. Using the power of asking, he's raised more than $2,500,000 in donations and enlisted more than 4,000 people to help him in his crusade.

When Chad realized he would need more barges, trucks, and equipment, he asked state and local officials for help, only to be turned down. Not to be dissuaded, Chad grabbed a phone book, turned to the business listings, and called Alcoa – "because," he said, "it started with an A."

Armed only with his passionate commitment to his dream, Chad asked to speak to the "top guy." Eventually

Alcoa gave him $8,400. Later, working his way through the A's, he called Anheuser-Busch. As reported in *Smithsonian* magazine, Mary Alice Ramirez, the director of environmental outreach at Anheuser-Busch, remembers her first conversation with Chad this way:

"Will you give me some money?" Chad asked.

"Who are you?" replied Ramirez.

"I want to get rid of the garbage in the Mississippi River," Chad said.

"Can you show me a proposal?" Ramirez inquired.

"What's a proposal?" Chad replied.

Ramirez eventually invited Chad to a meeting and gave him a check for $25,000 to expand his Mississippi River Beautification and Restoration Project.[1]

More important than Chad's knowledge of fund-raising was his clear desire to make a difference, his unflagging enthusiasm, his complete dedication to the project – and his willingness to ask.

Eventually, everything Chad needed was secured through asking. He now has a board of directors made up of lawyers, accountants, and corporate officers. He has several full-time staff members and thousands of volunteers.

In the process, he has not only cleaned up miles of shoreline on the Mississippi, Illinois, Anacostia, Potomac, Missouri, Ohio, and Rock Rivers – removing over 1 million tons of trash – but he's also drawn attention to the health and beauty of all rivers and the responsibility we all share in keeping them clean.[2]

Start Asking Today

Take time now to make a list of the things that you want that you don't ask for at home, school, or work. Next to each one, write down how you stop yourself from asking. What is your fear? Next, write down what it is costing you not to ask. Then write down what benefit you would get if you were to ask.

Take time to make a list of what you need to ask for in each of the following seven goal categories that I outlined in Principle 3 ("Decide What You Want"): financial, career, fun time and recreation, health, relationships, personal projects and hobbies, and contribution to the larger community (see pages 49–51). This might include a raise, a loan, seed money, feedback about your performance, a referral, an endorsement, time off to get additional training, someone to babysit your children, a massage, a hug, or help with a volunteer project.

Principle 16

Reject Rejection

We keep going back, stronger, not weaker,
because we will not allow rejection to beat us down.
It will only strengthen our resolve.
To be successful there is no other way.

Earl G. Graves – Founder and publisher of *Black Enterprise* magazine

If you are going to be successful, you are going to need to learn how to deal with rejection. Rejection is a natural part of life. You get rejected when you aren't picked for the team, don't get the part in the play, don't get elected, don't get into the college or graduate school of your choice, don't get the job or promotion you wanted, don't get the raise you wanted, don't get the appointment you requested, don't get the date you asked for, don't get the permission you requested, or get fired. You get rejected when your manuscript is rejected, your proposal is turned down, your new product idea is passed over, your fund-raising request is ignored, your design concept is not accepted, your application for membership is denied, or your offer of marriage is not accepted.

Rejection Is a Myth!

To get over rejection, you have to realize that rejection is really a myth. It doesn't really exist. It is simply a concept that you hold in your head. Think about it. If you ask Patty to have dinner with you and she says no, you didn't have anyone to eat dinner with before you asked her, and you don't have anyone to eat dinner with after you asked her. The situation didn't get worse; it stayed the same. It only gets worse if you go inside and tell yourself something extra like "See, Mother was right. No one will ever like me. I am the slug of the universe!"

If you apply to Harvard for graduate school and you don't get in, you weren't in Harvard before you applied, and you are not in Harvard after you applied. Again, your life didn't get worse; it stayed the same. You haven't really lost anything. And think about this – you have spent your whole life not going to Harvard; you know how to handle that.

The truth is, you never have anything to lose by asking, and because there is something to possibly gain, by all means ask.

SWSWSWSW

Whenever you ask anyone for anything, remember the following: SWSWSWSW, which stands for "some will, some won't; so what – someone's waiting." Some people are going to say yes, and some are going to say no. So what! Out there somewhere, someone is waiting for you and your ideas. It is simply a numbers game. You have to keep asking until you get a yes. The yes is out there waiting. As my partner Mark Victor Hansen is so fond of saying, "What you want wants you." You just have to hang in there long enough to eventually get a yes.

81 Nos, 9 Straight Yeses

Because it had so dramatically changed her life, a graduate of my "Self-Esteem and Peak Performance Seminar" was volunteering in the evenings to call people to enroll them in an upcoming seminar I was conducting in St. Louis. She made a commitment to talk to three people every night for a month. Many of the calls turned into long conversations with people asking tons of questions. She made a total of 90 phone calls. The first 81 people decided not to take the seminar. The next 9 people all signed up. She had a 10% success ratio, which is a good ratio for phone enrollments, but all 9 enrollments came in the last 9 calls. What if she had given up after the first 50 people and said, "This just isn't working. It's not worth the effort. Nobody is signing up." But because she had a dream of sharing with others the life-transforming experience that she had had, she persevered in the face of a lot of rejection, knowing that it was indeed a numbers game. And her commitment to the outcome paid off – she was instrumental in helping 9 people transform their lives.

If you're committed to a cause that evokes your passion and commitment, you keep learning from your experiences, and you stay the course to the end, you will eventually create your desired outcome.

> Never give up on your dream … Perseverance is all important. If you don't have the desire and the belief in yourself to keep trying after you've been told you should quit, you'll never make it.
>
> **Tawni O'Dell** – Author of *Back Roads,* an Oprah Book Club pick

Just Say "Next!"

Get used to the idea that there is going to be a lot of rejection along the way to the gold ring. The secret to success is to not give up. When someone says no, you say, *"Next!"* Keep on asking. When Colonel Harlan Sanders left home with his pressure cooker and his special recipe for cooking Southern fried chicken, he received over 300 rejections before he found someone to believe in his dream. Because he rejected rejection over 300 times, there are now 11,000 KFC restaurants in 80 countries around the world.

If one person tells you no, ask someone else. Remember, there are over 5 billion people on the planet! Someone, somewhere, sometime will say yes. Don't get stuck in your fear or resentment. Move on to the next person. It is a numbers game. Someone is waiting to say yes.

Chicken Soup for the Soul®

In the fall of 1991, Mark Victor Hansen and I began the process of selling our first *Chicken Soup for the Soul®* book to a publisher. We flew to New York with our agent, Jeff Herman, and met with every major publisher that would grant us a meeting. All of them said they weren't interested. "Collections of short stories don't sell." "There's no edge to the stories." "The title will never work." After that we were rejected by another 20 publishers who had received the manuscript through the mail. After being rejected by more than 30 publishers, our agent gave the book back to us and said, "I'm sorry; I can't sell it for you." What did we do? We said, *"Next!"*

We also knew we had to think outside of the box. After weeks of wracking our brains, we hit on an idea that we thought would work. We printed up a form that was a promise to buy the book when it was published. It included a place for people to write their name, address, and the number of books they pledged to buy.

Over a period of months, we asked everyone who attended our speeches or seminars to complete the form if they would buy a copy of the book when it was published. Eventually we had promises to buy 20,000 books.

The following spring, Mark and I attended the American

Booksellers Association convention in Anaheim, California, and walked from booth to booth, talking to any publisher who would listen. Even with copies of our signed pledge forms to demonstrate the market for our book, we were turned down again and again. But again and again we said, *"Next!"* At the end of the second very long day, we gave a copy of the first 30 stories in the book to Peter Vegso and Gary Seidler, copresidents of Health Communications, Inc., a struggling publisher specializing in addiction-and-recovery books, who agreed to take it home and look it over. Later that week, Gary Seidler took the manuscript to the beach and read it. He loved it and decided to give us a chance. Those hundreds of "nexts" had paid off! After over 130 rejections, that first book went on to sell 8 million copies, spawning a series of 80 best-selling books that have been translated into 39 languages.

And those pledge forms? When the book was finally published, we stapled an announcement to the signed forms, sent them to the person at the address on the form, and waited for a check. Almost everyone who had promised to buy a book came through on his or her commitment. In fact, one entrepreneur in Canada bought 1,700 copies and gave one to every one of his clients.

This manuscript of yours that has just come back from another editor is a precious package. Don't consider it rejected. Consider that you've addressed it "to the editor who can appreciate my work" and it has simply come back stamped "not at this address." Just keep looking for the right address.

Barbara Kingsolver – Best-selling author of *The Poisonwood Bible*

155 Rejections Didn't Stop Him

When 19-year-old Rick Little wanted to start a program in the high schools that would teach kids how to deal with their feelings, handle conflict, clarify their life goals, and learn communication skills and the values that would help them live more effective and fulfilling lives, he wrote a proposal and shopped it to over 155 foundations. He slept in the back of his car and ate peanut butter on crackers for the better part of a year. But he never gave up his dream. Eventually, the Kellogg Foundation gave Rick $130,000. (That's almost $1,000 for each no he endured.) Since that time, Rick and his team have raised over $100 million to implement the Quest program in over 30,000 schools around the world. Three million kids per year are being taught important life skills because one 19-year-old rejected rejection and kept on going until he got a yes.

In 1989 Rick received a grant for $65,000,000, the second largest grant ever given in U.S. history, to create the International Youth Foundation. What if Rick had given up after the one hundredth rejection and said to himself, *Well, I guess this just isn't supposed to be?* What a great loss to the world and to Rick's higher purpose for being.

He Knocked on 12,500 Doors

> I take rejection as someone blowing a bugle in my ear
> to wake me up and get going, rather than retreat.
>
> **Sylvester Stallone** – Actor, writer, and director

When Dr. Ignatius Piazza was a young chiropractor fresh
out of school, he decided he wanted to set up offices in
the Monterey Bay area of California. When he approached
the local chiropractic association for assistance they ad-
vised him to set up shop somewhere else. They told him
he wouldn't be successful because there were already too
many chiropractors in the area. Undaunted, he applied
the Next Principle. For months, he went from door to door
early in the morning until sunset, knocking on doors. After introducing himself as the new young doctor in town,
he asked a few questions:

"Where should I locate my office?"

"What newspapers should I advertise in to reach your
neighbors?"

"Should I open early in the morning or stay open into
the evening for those who have nine-to-five jobs?"

"Should I call my clinic Chiropractic West or Ignatius
Piazza Chiropractic?"

And finally, he asked, "When I hold my open house,
would you like to receive an invitation?" If people said
yes, he wrote down their names and addresses and continued on ... day after day, month after month. By the time

he was done, he had knocked on over 12,500 doors and talked to over 6,500 people. He got a lot of nos. He got a lot of nobody-homes. He even got trapped on one porch – cornered by a pit bull – for a whole afternoon! But he also received enough yeses that during his first month in practice he saw 233 new patients and earned a record income of $72,000 – in an area that "didn't need another chiropractor"!

Remember, to get what you want you are going to need to ask, ask, ask, and say *next, next, next* until you get the yes(es) you are looking for! Asking is, was, and always will be a numbers game. Don't take it personally, because it isn't personal. It's just not a match until it is.

Some Famous Rejections

> The girl doesn't, it seems to me, have a special perception or feeling which would lift that book above the "curiosity" level.
>
> From the rejection slip for *The Diary of Anne Frank*

Everyone who has ever made it to the top has had to endure rejections. You just have to realize that they are not personal. Consider the following:

- When Alexander Graham Bell offered the rights to the telephone for $100,000 to Carl Orton, president of

Western Union, Orton replied, "What use would this company make of an electrical toy?"

- Angie Everhart, who started modeling at the age of 16, was once told by model agency owner Eileen Ford that she would never make it as a model. Why not? "Red-heads don't sell." Everhart later became the first red-head in history to appear on the cover of *Glamour* magazine, had a great modeling career, and then went on to appear in 27 films and numerous TV shows.

- Novelist Stephen King almost made a multimillion-dollar mistake when he threw his *Carrie* manuscript in the garbage because he was tired of the rejections. "We are not interested in science fiction which deals with negative utopias," he was told. "They do not sell." Luckily, his wife fished it out of the garbage. Eventually *Carrie* was printed by another publisher, sold more than 4 million copies, and was made into a blockbuster film.

- In 1998, Google cofounders Sergey Brin and Larry Page approached Yahoo! and suggested a merger. Yahoo! could have snapped up the company for a handful of stock, but instead they suggested that the young Googlers keep working on their little school project and come back when they had grown up. Within 5 years, Google had an estimated market capitalization of $20 billion. At the time of this writing, they were about to launch an initial public offering auction that eventually raised $1.67 billion.

It is impossible to sell animal stories in the U.S.A.

From the rejection slip for George Orwell's *Animal Farm*

The record for the most astounding number of rejections would probably be John Creasey's. A popular British mystery writer, Creasey collected 743 rejection slips before he sold his first book! Impervious to rejection, over the next 40 years he went on to publish 562 full-length books under 28 different pseudonyms! If John Creasey can handle 743 rejections on his way to success, so can you.

Principle 17

Use Feedback to Your Advantage

Feedback is the breakfast of champions.

Ken Blanchard and **Spencer Johnson**
Coauthors of *The One Minute Manager*

Once you begin to take action, you'll start getting feedback about whether you're doing the right thing. You'll get data, advice, help, suggestions, direction, and even criticism that will help you constantly adjust and move forward while continually enhancing your knowledge, abilities, attitudes, and relationships. But asking for feedback is really only the first part of the equation. Once you receive feedback, you have to be willing to respond to it.

There Are Two Kinds of Feedback

There are two kinds of feedback you might encounter – negative and positive. We tend to prefer the positive – that is, results, money, praise, a raise, a promotion, satisfied customers, awards, happiness, inner peace, intimacy, pleasure. It feels better. It tells us that we are on course, that we are doing the right thing.

We tend not to like negative feedback – lack of results, little or no money, criticism, poor evaluations, being passed over for a raise or a promotion, complaints, unhappiness, inner conflict, loneliness, pain. However, there is as much useful data in negative feedback as there is in positive feedback. It tells us that we are off course, headed in the wrong direction, doing the wrong thing. That is also valuable information.

In fact, it's so valuable that one of the most useful projects you could undertake is to change how you feel about negative feedback. I like to refer to negative feedback as information about "improvement opportunities." The world is telling me where and how I can improve what I am doing. Here is a place I can get better. Here is where I can correct my behavior to get even closer to what I say I want – more money, more sales, a promotion, a better relationship, better grades, or more success on the athletic field.

To reach your goals more quickly, you need to welcome, receive, and embrace all the feedback that comes your way.

On Course, Off Course, On Course, Off Course

There are many ways to respond to feedback, some of which work (they take you closer to your stated objectives), and some of which don't (they keep you stuck or take you even further from your goals).

When I conduct trainings on the success principles, I illustrate this point by asking for a volunteer from the audience to stand at the far side of the room. The volunteer represents the goal I want to reach. My task is to walk across the room to where he is standing. If I get to where he is standing, I have successfully reached my goal.

I instruct the volunteer to act as a constant feedback-generating machine. Every time I take a step, he is to say "On course" if I am walking directly toward him and "Off course" if I am walking even the slightest bit off to either side.

Then I begin to walk very slowly toward the volunteer. Every time I take a step directly toward him, the volunteer says, "On course." Every few steps, I purposely veer off course, and the volunteer says, "Off course." I immediately correct my direction. Every few steps, I veer off course again and then correct again in response to his "Off course" feedback. After a lot of zigzagging, I eventually reach my goal ... and give the person a hug for volunteering.

I ask the audience to tell me which the volunteer had

said more often – "On course" or "Off course." The answer is always "Off course." And here is the interesting part. I was off course more than I was on course, and I still got there … just by continually taking action and constantly adjusting to the feedback. The same is true in life. All we have to do is to start to take action and then respond to the feedback. If we do that diligently enough and long enough, we will eventually get to our goals and achieve our dreams.

Ways of Responding to Feedback That Don't Work

Though there are many ways you can respond to feedback, some responses simply don't work:

1. **Caving in and quitting:** As part of the seminar exercise I described above, I will repeat the process of walking toward my goal; however, in this round I will purposely veer off course, and when my volunteer keeps repeating "Off course" over and over, I break down and cry, "I can't take it anymore. Life is too hard. I can't take all this negative criticism. I quit!"

   How many times have you or someone you know received negative feedback and simply caved in over it? All that does is keep you stuck in the same place.

   It's easier not to cave in when you receive feedback

if you remember that feedback is simply information. Think of it as correctional guidance instead of criticism. Think of the automatic pilot system on an airplane. The system is constantly telling the plane that it has gone too high, too low, too far to the right, or too far to the left. The plane just keeps correcting in response to the feedback it is receiving. It doesn't all of a sudden freak out and break down because of the relentless flow of feedback. Stop taking feedback so personally. It is just information designed to help you adjust and get to your goal a whole lot faster.

2. **Getting mad at the source of the feedback:** Once again, I will begin walking toward the other end of the room while purposely veering off course, causing the volunteer to say "Off course" over and over. This time I put one hand on my hip, stick out my chin, point my finger, and yell, "Bitch, bitch, bitch! All you ever do is criticize me! You're so negative. Why can't you ever say anything positive?"

   Think about it. How many times have you reacted with anger and hostility toward someone who was giving you feedback that was genuinely useful? All it does is push the person and the feedback away.

3. **Ignoring the feedback:** For my third demonstration, imagine me putting my fingers in my ears and determinedly walking off course. The volunteer might be saying "Off course, off course," but I can't hear anything because my fingers are in my ears.

   Not listening to or ignoring the feedback is another

response that doesn't work. We all know people who tune out everyone's point of view but their own. They are simply not interested in what other people think. They don't want to hear anything anyone else has to say. The sad thing is, feedback could significantly transform their lives, if only they would only listen.

So, as you can see, when someone gives you feedback, there are three possible reactions that don't work: (1) crying, falling apart, caving in, and giving up; (2) getting angry at the source of the feedback; and (3) not listening to or ignoring the feedback.

Crying and falling apart is simply ineffective. It may temporarily release whatever emotions you have built up in your system, but it takes you out of the game. It doesn't get you anywhere. It simply immobilizes you. Not a great success strategy! Caving in and giving up doesn't work either. It may make you feel safer and may stop the flow of "negative" feedback, but it doesn't get you the good stuff! You can't win in the game of life if you are not on the playing field!

Getting angry at the person giving you the feedback is equally ineffective! It just makes the source of the valuable feedback attack you back or simply go away. What good is that? It may temporarily make you feel better, but it doesn't help you get more successful.

On the third day of my advanced seminar, when everyone knows everybody else pretty well, I have the whole group (about 40 people) stand up, mill around, and ask as many people as possible the following question: "How do you see me limiting myself?" After doing this for 30 minutes, people sit down and record what they have heard. You'd think that this would be hard to listen to for 30 minutes, but it is such valuable feedback that people are actually grateful for the opportunity to become aware of their limiting behaviors and replace them with successful behaviors. Everyone then develops an action plan for transcending their limiting behavior.

Remember, feedback is simply information. You don't have to take it personally. Just welcome it and use it. The most intelligent and productive response is to say, "Thank you for the feedback. Thank you for caring enough to take the time to tell me what you see and how you feel. I appreciate it."

Ask for Feedback

Most people will not voluntarily give you feedback. They are as uncomfortable with possible confrontation as you are. They don't want to hurt your feelings. They are afraid of your reaction. They don't want to risk your disapproval. So to get honest and open feedback, you are going to need to ask for it ... and make it safe for the person to give it to you. In other words, don't shoot the messenger.

A powerful question to ask family members, friends, and colleagues is "How do you see me limiting myself?" You might think that the answers would be hard to listen to, but most people find the information so valuable that they are grateful for what people tell them. Armed with this new feedback, they can create a plan of action for replacing their limiting behaviors with more effective and productive behaviors.

The Most Valuable Question You May Ever Learn

In the 1980s, a multimillionaire businessman taught me a question that radically changed the quality of my life. If the only thing you get out of reading this book is the consistent use of this question in your personal and business life, it will have been worth the money and time you have invested. So what is this magical question that can improve the quality of every relationship you are in, every product you produce, every service you deliver, every meeting you conduct, every class you teach, and every transaction you enter into? Here it is:

> On a scale of 1 to 10, how would you rate the quality
> of our relationship (service/product) during the last week
> (2 weeks/month/quarter/semester/season)?

Here are a number of variations on the same question that have served me well over the years:

On a scale of 1 to 10, how would you rate the meeting we just had? me as a manager? me as a parent? me as a teacher? this class? this meal? my cooking? our sex life? this deal? this book?

Any answer less than a 10 gets the follow-up question:

What would it take to make it a 10?

This is where the valuable information comes from. Knowing that a person is dissatisfied is not enough. Knowing in detail what will satisfy them gives you the information you need to do what is necessary to create a winning product, service, or relationship.

Make it a habit to end every project, meeting, class, training, consultation, installation, and consultation with the two questions.

Make It a Weekly Ritual

I ask my wife these same two questions every Sunday night. Here is a typical scenario:

"How would you rate the quality of our relationship this past week?"

"Eight."

"What would it take to make it a ten?"

"Put the kids to bed without me having to remind you that it's time to do it. Come in for dinner on time or call me and tell me you are going to be late. I hate sitting here waiting and wondering. Let me finish a joke I am telling without interrupting and taking over because you think you can tell it better. Put your dirty laundry in the clothes hamper instead of in a pile on the floor."

I also ask my assistants this question every Friday afternoon. Here is one response I received from Deborah early on in her employment:

"Six."

"Whoa! What would it take to make it a ten?"

"We were supposed to have a meeting this week to go over my quarterly review, but it got pushed aside by other matters. It makes me feel unimportant and that you don't care about me as much as the other people around here. I need to talk to you about a lot of things, and I feel really discounted. The other thing is that I feel that you are not using me enough. You are not delegating anything but the simple stuff to me. I want more responsibility. I want you to trust me more with the important stuff. I need more of a challenge. This job has become boring and uninteresting to me. I need more of a challenge, or I am not going to make it here."

This was not easy to hear, but it was true and it led to two wonderful results. It helped me delegate more "important stuff" to her and thus cleared my plate, giving me more free time – and it also created a happier assistant who was able to serve me and the company better.

Be Willing to Ask

Most people are afraid to ask for corrective feedback because they are afraid of what they are going to hear. There is nothing to be afraid of. The truth is the truth. You are better off knowing the truth than not knowing the truth. Once you know it, you can do something about it. You cannot fix what you don't know is broken. You cannot improve your life, your relationships, your game, or your performance without feedback.

But what's the worst part of this avoidance approach to life? You are the only one who is not in on the secret. The other person has usually already told their spouse, their friends, their parents, their business associates, and other potential customers what they are dissatisfied with. As we discussed in Principle 1 ("Take 100% Responsibility for Your Life"), most people would rather complain than take constructive action to solve their problems. The only problem is that they are complaining to the wrong person. They should be telling you, but they are unwilling to for fear of your reaction. As a result, you are being deprived of the very thing you need to improve your relationship, your product, your service, your teaching, or your parenting. You must do two things to remedy this.

First, you must intentionally and actively solicit feedback. Ask your partner, your friends, your colleagues, your boss, your employees, your clients, your parents, your teachers, your students, and your coaches. Use the question frequently. Make it a habit to always ask for corrective feedback. "What can I/we do to make this better? What would it take to make it a ten for you?"

Second, you must be grateful for the feedback. Do not get defensive. Just say, "Thank you for caring enough to share that with me!" If you are truly grateful for the feedback, you will get a reputation for being open to feedback. Remember, feedback is a gift that helps you be more effective.

Be grateful for it.

Get your head out of the sand and ask, ask, ask! Then check in with yourself to see what fits for you, and put the useful feedback into action. Take whatever steps are necessary to improve the situation – including changing your own behavior.

A few years ago, our company discontinued using a printer because another one offered us better service for a lower price. About 4 months later, our original printer called and said, "I've noticed you haven't used me for any printing lately. What would it take for you to start giving me your printing business again?"

I replied, "Lower prices, on-time turnaround, and pickup and delivery. If you can guarantee us those three things, I'll give you a small portion of our printing and try you again." Eventually, he won back most of our printing because he beat other people's prices, picked up and delivered, finished on time, and provided more than acceptable quality. Because he asked the question "What would it take … ?" he got the information he needed to ensure his ongoing success with us.

She Asked Her Way to Success in 3 Short Months

One of the best-selling weight-loss books ever published was the book *Thin Thighs in 30 Days*. What's so interesting about it, though, is that it was developed solely using feedback. The author, Wendy Stehling, worked in an advertising agency but hated her job. She wanted to start her own agency but didn't have the money to do so. She knew she would need about $100,000, so she began asking, "What's the quickest way to raise $100,000?"

Sell a book, said the feedback.

She decided if she wrote a book that could sell 100,000 copies in 90 days – and she made $1 per book – she would raise the $100,000 she needed. But what kind of book would 100,000 people want? "Well, what are the best-selling books in America?" she asked.

Weight loss books, said the feedback.

"Yes, but how would I distinguish myself as an expert?" she asked.

Ask other women, said the feedback.

So she went out to the marketplace and asked, "If you could lose weight in only one part of your body, what part would you choose?" The overwhelming response from women was *My thighs*.

"When would you want to lose it?" she asked.

Around April or May, in time for swimsuit season, said the feedback.

So what did she do? She wrote a book called *Thin Thighs in 30 Days* and released it April 15. By June, she had her $100,000 – all because she asked people what they wanted and responded to the feedback by giving it to them.

How to Look Really Brilliant with Little Effort

Virginia Satir, the author of the classic parenting book *Peoplemaking*, was probably the most successful and famous family therapist that ever lived.

During her long and illustrious career, she was hired by the Michigan State Department of Social Services to provide a proposal on how to revamp and restructure the Department of Social Services so it would serve the client population better. Sixty days later, she provided the department with a 150-page report, which they said was the most amazing piece of work they had ever seen. "This is brilliant!" they gushed. "How did you come up with all these ideas?"

She replied, "Oh, I just went out to all the social workers in your system and I asked them what it would take for the system to work better."

Listen to the Feedback

> Human beings were given a left foot and a right foot to make a mistake first to the left, then to the right, left again and repeat.

Buckminster Fuller – Engineer, inventor, and philosopher

Whether we ask or not, feedback comes to us in various forms. It might come verbally from a colleague. Or it might be a letter from the government. It might be the bank refusing your loan. Or it could be a special opportunity that comes your way because of a specific step you took.

Whatever it is, it's important to listen to the feedback. Simply take a step … and listen. Take another step and listen. If you hear "Off course," take a step in a direction you believe may be on course … and listen. Listen externally to what others may be telling you, but also listen internally to what your body, your feelings, and your instincts may be telling you.

Is your mind and body saying, "I'm happy; I like this; this is the right job for me," or "I'm weary; I'm emotionally drained; I don't like this as much as I thought; I don't have a good feeling about that guy"?

Whatever feedback you get, don't ignore the yellow alerts. Never go against your gut. If it doesn't feel right to you, it probably isn't.

Is All Feedback Accurate?

Not all feedback is useful or accurate. You must consider the source. Some feedback is polluted by the psychological distortions of the person giving you the feedback. For example, if your drunk husband tells you, "You are a no-good *bleep*," that is probably not accurate or useful feedback. The fact that your husband is drunk and angry, however, *is feedback you should listen to*.

Look for Patterns

Additionally, you should look for patterns in the feedback you get. As my friend Jack Rosenblum likes to say: "If one person tells you you're a horse, they're crazy. If three people tell you you're a horse, there's a conspiracy afoot. If ten people tell you you're a horse, it's time to buy a saddle."

The point is that if several people are telling you the same thing, there is probably some truth in it. Why resist it? You may think you get to be right, but the question you have to ask yourself is "Would I rather be right or be happy? Would I rather be right or be successful?"

I have a friend who would rather be right than be happy and successful. He got mad at anyone who tried to give him feedback. "Don't you talk to me that way, young lady." "Don't tell me how to run my business. This is my business and I'll run it the way I want to." "I don't give a hoot what you think." He was a "my way or the highway" person. He wasn't interested in anyone else's opinion or feedback. In the process, he alienated his wife, his two daughters, his clients, and all his employees. He ended up with two divorces, kids who didn't want to speak to him, and two bankrupt businesses. But he was "right." So be it, but don't *you* get caught in this trap. It is a dead-end street.

What feedback have you been receiving from your family, friends, members of the opposite sex, coworkers, boss, partners, clients, vendors, and your body that you need to pay more attention to? Are there any patterns that stand out? Make a list, and next to each item, write an action step you can take to get back on course.

What to Do When the Feedback Tells You You've Failed

When all indicators say you've had a "failure experience," there are a number of things you can do to respond appropriately and keep moving forward:

1. Acknowledge you did the best you could with the awareness, knowledge, and skills you had at the time.
2. Acknowledge that you survived and that you can absolutely cope with any and all of the consequences or results.

3. Write down everything you learned from the experience. Write all of your insights and lessons down in a file in your computer or a journal called *Insights and Lessons*. Read through this file often. Ask others involved – your family, team, employees, clients, and others – what they learned. I often have my staff write "I learned that ..." at the top of a piece of paper and then write as much as they can think of in a 5-minute period. Then we make a list under the heading of "Ways to Do It Better Next Time."

4. Make sure to thank everyone for their feedback and their insights. If someone is hostile in the delivery of their feedback, remember that it is an expression of their level of fear, not your level of incompetence or unlovability. Again, just thank them for their feedback. Explaining, justifying, and blaming are all a waste of everybody's time. Just take in the feedback, use whatever is applicable and valuable for the future, and discard the rest.

5. Clean up any messes that have been created and deliver any communications that are necessary to complete the experience – including any apologies or regrets that are due. Do not try to hide the failure.

6. Take some time to go back and review your successes. It's important to remind yourself that you have had many more successes than you have had failures. You've done many more things right than you've done wrong.

7. Regroup. Spend some time with positive loving friends,

family, and coworkers who can reaffirm your worth and your contribution.

8. Refocus on your vision. Incorporate the lessons learned, recommit to your original plan, or create a new plan of action, and then get on with it. Stay in the game. Keep moving toward the fulfillment of your dreams. You're going to make a lot of mistakes along the way. Dust yourself off, get back on your horse, and keep riding.

Principle 18

Commit to Constant and Never-Ending Improvement

We have an innate desire to endlessly learn, grow, and develop. We want to become more than what we already are. Once we yield to this inclination for continuous and never-ending improvement, we lead a life of endless accomplishments and satisfaction.

Chuck Gallozzi

People call me a perfectionist, but I'm not. I'm a "rightist." I do something until it's right, and then I move on to the next thing.

James Cameron – Oscar-winning director of *Titanic* and the *Terminator* series

In Japan, the word for constant and never-ending improvement is *kaizen*. Not only is this an operating philosophy for modern Japanese businesses, it is also the age-old philosophy of warriors, too – and it's become the personal mantra of millions of successful people.

Achievers – whether in business, sports, or the arts – are

committed to continual improvement. If you want to be more successful, you need to learn to ask yourself, "How can I make this better? How can I do it more efficiently? How can I do this more profitably? How can we do this with greater love?"

The Mind-Numbing Pace of Change

In today's world, a certain amount of improvement is necessary just to keep up with the rapid pace of change. New technologies are announced nearly every month. New manufacturing techniques are discovered even more often. New words come into use anytime a trend or fad catches on. And what we learn about ourselves, about our health, and about the capacity for human thought continues almost unabated.

Improving is therefore necessary simply to survive. But to thrive, as successful people do, a more dedicated approach to improvement is required.

Improve in Small Increments

Whenever you set out to improve your skills, change your behavior, or better your family life or business, beginning in small, manageable steps gives you a greater chance of long-term success. Doing too much too fast not only over-whelms you (or anyone else involved in the improve-ment), it can doom the effort to failure – thereby reinforcing the belief that it's difficult, if not impossible, to succeed. When you start with small, achievable steps you can easily master, it reinforces your belief that you can easily improve.

Decide What to Improve On

At work, your goal might be for your company to improve the quality of your product or service, your customer ser-vice program, or your advertising. Professionally you might want to improve your computer skills, your typing speed, your sales skills, or your negotiating skills. At home you might want to improve your parenting skills, com-munication skills, or cooking skills. You could also focus on improving your health and fitness, your knowledge of investing and money management, or your piano play-ing. Or perhaps you want to develop greater inner peace through meditation, yoga, and prayer. Whatever your goal, decide where you want to improve and what steps you'll need to take to achieve that improvement.

Is it learning a new skill? Perhaps you can find that in a night class at the local community college. If it's improv-ing your service to the community, perhaps you can find a way to spend an extra hour per week volunteering.

To keep yourself focused on constant and never-ending

improvement, ask yourself every day, "How can I/we improve today? What can I/we do better than before? Where can I learn a new skill or develop a new competency?" If you do, you'll embark on a lifelong journey of improvement that will ensure your success.

You Can't Skip Steps

He who stops being better stops being good.
Oliver Cromwell – British politician and soldier (1599–1658)

One of life's realities is that major improvements take time; they don't happen overnight. But because so many of today's products and services promise overnight perfection, we've come to expect instant gratification – and we become discouraged when it doesn't happen. However, if you make a commitment to learning something new every day, getting just a little bit better every day, then eventually – over time – you will reach your goals.

Becoming a master takes time. You have to practice, practice, practice! You have to hone your skills through constant use and refinement. It takes years to have the depth and breadth of experience that produces expertise, insight, and wisdom. Every book you read, every class you take, every experience you have is another building block in your career and your life.

Don't shortchange yourself by not being ready when

your big break appears. Make sure you have done your homework and honed your craft. Actors usually have to do a lot of preparation – acting classes, community theater, off-Broadway plays, bit parts in movies and television, more acting classes, voice lessons, accent training, dancing lessons, martial arts training, learning to ride a horse, more bit parts – until one day they are ready for the dream part that is ready for them.

Successful basketball players learn to shoot with their opposite hand, improve their foul-throw shooting, and work on their three-point shots. Artists experiment with different media. Airline pilots train for every kind of emergency in a flight simulator. Doctors go back to school to learn new procedures and obtain advanced certifications. They are all engaged in a process of constant and never-ending improvement.

Make a commitment to keep getting better and better every day in every way. If you do, you'll enjoy the feelings of increased self-esteem and self-confidence that come from self-improvement, as well as the ultimate success that will inevitably follow.

Margin of Greatness

In the sport of professional baseball most respectable players bat an average of .250, or 1 hit for every 4 times they come to bat. If a .250 batter is also a good fielder, he can expect to do well in the majors. But anyone who hits

.300, or 3 hits for every 10 times he comes to bat, is considered a star. By the end of a season, out of the thousands of players in the leagues, only about a dozen players will have achieved a .300 average. These hitters are honored as the greatest players, receive the multimillion-dollar player contracts, and land the lucrative commercial endorsements.

But consider this: The difference between the truly great ones and the average players is only 1 hit out of 20! A player who bats .250 gets 5 hits in every 20 times at bat, but a .300 hitter gets 6 hits out of those same 20 times at bat. Isn't that amazing? In the world of professional baseball, the margin of greatness is only 1 more hit out of 20! It takes only a little extra bit of performance to go from good to great.

Practice Persistence

Most people give up just when they're about
to achieve success. They quit on the one-yard line.
They give up at the last minute of the game,
one foot from a winning touchdown.

H. Ross Perot – American billionaire
and former U.S. presidential candidate

Persistence is probably the single most common quality of
high achievers. They simply refuse to give up. The longer
you hang in there, the greater the chance that something
will happen in your favor. No matter how hard it seems,
the longer you persist the more likely your success.

It's Not Always Going to Be Easy

Sometimes you are going to have to persist in the face of
obstacles – unseen obstacles – that no amount of planning or forethought could have predicted. Sometimes,
you'll encounter what seem like overwhelming odds. And
sometimes, the universe will test your commitment to the

goal you're pursuing. The going may be hard, requiring you to refuse to give up while you learn new lessons, develop new parts of yourself, and make difficult decisions.

> History has demonstrated that the most notable winners usually encountered heartbreaking obstacles before they triumphed. They won because they refused to become discouraged by their defeats.
>
> **B.C. Forbes** – Founder of *Forbes* magazine

Hugh Panero, chief executive at XM Satellite Radio, is an example of amazing commitment and perseverance in the corporate sector. After 2 years recruiting investors ranging from General Motors and Hughes Electronics to DIRECTV and Clear Channel Communications, Panero's dream of becoming the world's largest subscription radio service nearly collapsed at the last minute when investors threatened to back out if an acceptable deal wasn't struck by midnight, June 6, 2000. After exhausting negotiations and shuttle diplomacy, Panero and his chairman of the board, Gary Parsons, secured commitments of $225 million just minutes before the deadline.

Less than a year later, the launch of one of XM's $200 million satellites was aborted just 11 seconds before liftoff when an engineer misread a message on his computer screen, forcing the company to wait for the next available launch date 2 months later!

Still, Panero persevered and finally scheduled the

debut of XM Radio's 101 channels of programming for September 12, 2001. But when terrorists attacked the World Trade Center on the morning of September 11 – just a day prior to the scheduled debut – Panero was forced to cancel the satellite's launch party and pull XM's inaugural TV ad featuring a rap star rocketing past a group of towering skyscrapers.

Panero's team urged him to postpone the company's launch for another year. Yet in the end, Panero held fast to his dream and debuted the service just 2 weeks later.

Today, through all the setbacks and delays, most of which make our own daily difficulties pale by comparison, XM dominates the satellite radio business with more than 1.7 million subscribers paying every month to enjoy 68 channels of commercial-free music plus 33 channels of premier sports, talk, comedy, children's and entertainment programming, and traffic and weather information. And stock prices have risen from the original price of $12 to $25 a share.[1]

Just One More Telephone Pole

Fall down seven times, get up eight times.

Japanese proverb

Having lost his right leg to cancer, Terry Fox embarked
on a cross-Canada run called the Marathon of Hope in
1980 to raise money for cancer research. His shuffle-and-
hop running style took him about 24 miles per day – close
to a complete 26-mile marathon every single day – with an
artificial leg! He managed to run for 143 days and covered
3,339 miles from his starting point in St. John's, New-
foundland, to Thunder Bay, Ontario, where he was forced
to abandon his run when doctors discovered cancer in his
lungs. He died a few months later, but his inspiring example has left a legacy: Annual Terry Fox runs are held in
Canada and around the world that so far have raised $340
million for cancer research. When asked how he kept
himself going as exhaustion set in and he had thousands
of miles ahead of him, he answered, "I just keep running
to the next telephone pole."

Five Years

"No" is a word on your path to "Yes." Don't give up too soon. Not even if well-meaning parents, relatives, friends, and colleagues tell you to get "a real job." Your dreams are your real job.

Joyce Spizer – Author of *Rejections of the Written Famous*

When Debbie Macomber decided to pursue her dream of becoming a writer, she rented a typewriter, put it on the kitchen table, and began typing each morning after the kids went off to school. When the kids came home, she moved the typewriter and made them dinner. When they went to bed, she moved it back and typed some more. For 2½ years, Debbie followed this routine. Supermom had become a struggling writer, and she was loving every minute of it.

One night, however, her husband, Wayne, sat her down and said, "Honey, I'm sorry, but you're not bringing in any income. We can't do this anymore. We can't survive on just what I make."

That night, her heart broken and her mind too busy to let her sleep, she stared at the ceiling in their darkened bedroom. Debbie knew – with all the responsibilities of keeping up a house and taking four kids to sports, church, and scouts – that working 40 hours a week would leave her no time to write.

Sensing her despair, her husband woke up and asked, "What's wrong?"

"I really think I could've made it as a writer. I really do."

Wayne was silent for a long time, then sat up, turned on the light, and said, "All right, honey, go for it."

So Debbie returned to her dream and her typewriter on the kitchen table, pounding out page after page for another 2½ years. Her family went without vacations, pinched pennies, and wore hand-me-downs.

But the sacrifice and the persistence finally paid off. After 5 years of struggling, Debbie sold her first book. Then another. And another. Until finally, today, Debbie has published more than 100 books, many of which have become *New York Times* best-sellers and 3 of which have sold for movies. Over 60 million copies of her books are in print, and she has millions of loyal fans.

And Wayne? All that sacrifice in support of his wife paid off handsomely. He got to retire at age 50 and now spends his time building an airplane in the basement of their 7,000-square-foot mansion.

Debbie's kids got a gift far more important than a few summer camps. As adults, they realize what Debbie gave them was far more important – permission and encouragement to pursue their own dreams.

Today, Debbie still has dreams she wants to fulfill – a television series based on her books, an Emmy Award, a number-one *New York Times* best seller.

To accomplish them, she has a routine: She gets up every morning at 4:30, reads her Bible, and writes in her journal. By 6:00, she's swimming laps in the pool. And by 7:30, she's in her office answering mail. She writes between 10:00 am and 4:00 pm, producing three new books a year with discipline and perseverance.

What could you accomplish if you were to follow your heart, practice this much daily discipline, and never give up?

Never Give Up on Your Hopes and Dreams

Persistence and determination alone are omnipotent. The slogan "press on" has solved and always will solve the problems of the human race.

Calvin Coolidge – Thirtieth president of the United States

Consider this:

- Admiral Robert Peary attempted to reach the North Pole seven times before he made it on try number eight.
- In its first 28 attempts to send rockets into space, NASA had 20 failures.
- Oscar Hammerstein had five flop shows that lasted less than a combined total of 6 weeks before *Oklahoma!* which ran for 269 weeks and grossed $7 million.
- Tawni O'Dell's career as a writer is a testament to her perseverance. After 13 years, she had written six unpublished novels and collected 300 rejection slips. Finally, her first novel, *Back Roads*, was published in

January 2000. Oprah Winfrey chose her book for the Oprah Book Club, and the newly anointed novel rose to number two on the *New York Times* Best-Seller List, where it remained for 8 weeks.

Never, Never, Never Give Up

During the Vietnam War, Texas computer billionaire H. Ross Perot decided he would give a Christmas present to every American prisoner of war in Vietnam. According to David Frost, who tells the story, Perot had thousands of packages wrapped and prepared for shipping. He chartered a fleet of Boeing 707s to deliver them to Hanoi, but the war was at its height, and the Hanoi government said it would refuse to cooperate. No charity was possible, officials explained, while American bombers were devastating Vietnamese villages. Perot offered to hire an American construction firm to help rebuild what Americans had knocked down. The government still wouldn't cooperate. Christmas drew near, and the packages were unsent. Refusing to give up, Perot finally took off in his chartered fleet and flew to Moscow, where his aides mailed the packages, one at a time, at the Moscow central post office. They were delivered intact.[2] Can you now see why this man became the great success that he did? He simply refused to ever quit.

Hang in There

It's always too soon to quit!

Norman Vincent Peale – Inspirational author

If you hang in there long enough, you will eventually reach your goal. Consider the career of major league baseball player Pat Tabler. Pat played 7 seasons in the minor leagues and 10 full seasons in the major leagues. He played in one World Series and one all-star game. When you look at his stats, it doesn't look like he was doing very well his first 7 years, but look at how his earnings grew over the lifetime of his career because he persevered in the pursuit of his dream.

	SALARY	BATTING AVERAGE
Minor Leagues		
1976	$2,500	.231
1977	$3,000	.238
1978	$3,500	.273
1979	$4,750	.316
1980	$5,000	.296
1981	$15,000	.301
1982	$25,000	.342
Cleveland Indians		
1983	$51,000	.291
1984	$102,000	.290
1985	$275,000	.275
1986	$470,000	.326
1987	$605,000	.307
Cleveland Indians, Kansas City Royals, and New York Mets		
1988	$800,000	.282
1989	$825,000	.259
1990	$725,000	.273
Toronto Blue Jays		
1991	$800,000	.216
1992	$800,000	.252
Total	**$5,546,750**	

How to Deal with Obstacles

For every failure, there's an alternative course of action. You just have to find it. When you come to a roadblock, take a detour.

Mary Kay Ash – Founder, Mary Kay Cosmetics

Whenever you confront an obstacle or run into a road-block, you need to stop and brainstorm three ways to get around, over, or through the block. For every obstacle, come up with three different strategies for handling the potential obstacle. There are any number of ways that will work, but you will find them only if you spend time looking for them. Always be solution-oriented in your thinking. Persevere until you find a way that works.

Difficulties are opportunities to better things; they are stepping-stones to greater experience. … When one door closes, another always opens; as a natural law it has to, to balance.

Brian Adams

Principle 20

Practice the Rule of Five

Success is the sum of small efforts,
repeated day in and day out.

Robert Collier – Best-selling author
and publisher of *The Secret of the Ages*

When Mark Victor Hansen and I published the first *Chicken Soup for the Soul*® book, we were so eager and committed to making it a best seller that we asked 15 best-selling authors ranging from John Gray (*Men Are from Mars, Women Are from Venus*) and Barbara DeAngelis (*Real Moments*) to Ken Blanchard (*The One Minute Manager*) and Scott Peck (*The Road Less Traveled*) for their guidance and advice. We received a ton of valuable information about what to do and how to do it. Next, we visited with book publishing and marketing guru Dan Poynter, who gave us even more great information. Then we bought and read John Kremer's *1001 Ways to Market Your Book*.

After all of that, we were overwhelmed with possibilities. To tell the truth, we became a little crazy. We didn't know where to start, plus we both had our speaking and seminar businesses to run.

Five Specific Things That Move You Toward Your Goal

We sought the advice of Ron Scolastico, a wonderful teacher, who told us, "If you would go every day to a very large tree and take five swings at it with a very sharp ax, eventually, no matter how large the tree, it would have to come down." How very simple and how very true! Out of that we developed what we have called the Rule of five. This simply means that every day, we do five specific things that will move our goal toward completion.

With the goal of getting *Chicken Soup for the Soul*® to the top of the *New York Times* Best-Seller List, it meant having five radio interviews or sending out five review copies to editors who might review the book or calling five network marketing companies and asking them to buy the book as a motivational tool for their salespeople or giving a seminar to at least five people and selling the book in the back of the room. On some days we would simply send out five free copies to people listed in the *Celebrity Address Book* – people such as Harrison Ford, Barbra Streisand, Paul McCartney, Steven Spielberg, and Sidney Poitier. As a result of that one activity, I ended up meeting Sidney Poitier – at his request – and we later learned that the producer of the television show *Touched by an Angel* required all of the people working on the show to read *Chicken Soup for the Soul*® to put them in "the right frame of mind." One day we sent copies of the book to all the jurors in the O.J. Simpson trial. A week later, we received a nice letter from Judge Lance Ito thanking us for thinking of the jurors, who were sequestered and not allowed to watch television or read the newspaper. The next day, four of the jurors were spotted reading the book by the press, and that led to some valuable public relations for the book.

We made phone calls to people who could review the book, we wrote press releases, we called in to talk shows (some at 3 am), we gave away free copies at our talks, we sent them to ministers to use as a source of talks for their sermons, we gave free "Chicken Soup for the Soul" talks at churches, we did book signings at any bookstore that would have us, we asked businesses to make bulk purchases for their employees, we got the book into the PXs on military bases, we asked our fellow speakers to sell the book at their talks, we asked seminar companies to put it in their catalogues, we bought a directory of catalogues and asked all the appropriate ones to carry the book, we visited gift shops and card shops and asked them to carry the book – we even got gas stations, bakeries, and restaurants to sell the book. It was a lot of effort – a minimum of five things a day, every day, day in and day out – for over 2 years.

Look What a Sustained Effort Can Do

Was it worth it? Yes! The book eventually sold over 8 million copies in 39 languages.

Did it happen overnight? No! We did not make a best seller list until over a year after the book came out – a year! But it was the sustained effort of the Rule of 5 for over 2 years that led to the success – one action at a time, one book at a time, one reader at a time. But slowly, over time, each reader told another reader, and eventually, like a slow-building chain letter, the word was spread and the book became a huge success – what *Time* magazine called "the publishing phenomenon of the decade." It was less of a publishing phenomenon and more of a phenomenon of persistent effort – thousands of individual activities that all added up to one large success.

In *Chicken Soup for the Gardener's Soul*, Jaroldeen Edwards describes the day her daughter Carolyn took her to Lake Arrowhead to see a wonder of nature – fields and fields of daffodils that extend for as far as the eye can see. From the top of the mountain, sloping down for many acres across folds and valleys, between the trees and bushes, following the terrain, there are rivers of daffodils in radiant bloom – a literal carpet of every hue of the color yellow, from the palest ivory to the deepest lemon to the most vivid salmon-orange. There appear to be over a million daffodil bulbs planted in this beautiful natural scene. It takes your breath away.

As they hiked into the center of this magical place, they eventually stumbled on a sign that read: "Answers to the Questions I Know You Are Asking." The first answer was "One Woman – Two Hands, Two Feet and Very Little Brain." The second was "One at a Time." The third: "Started in 1958."

One woman had forever changed the world over a 40-year period one bulb at a time. What might you accomplish if you were to do a little bit – five things – every day for the next 40 years toward the accomplishment of your goal. If you wrote 5 pages a day, that would be 73,000 pages of text – the equivalent of 243 books of 300 pages each. If you saved $5 a day, that would be $73,000, enough for four round-the-world trips! If you invested $5 a day, with compound interest at only 6% a year, at the end of 40 years, you'd have amassed a small fortune of around $305,000.

The Rule of five. Pretty powerful little principle, wouldn't you agree?

Principle 21

Surround Yourself with Successful People

You are the average of the five people
you spend the most time with.

Jim Rohn – Self-made millionaire and successful author

When Tim Ferriss was 12 years old, an unidentified caller left the above Jim Rohn quote on his answering machine. It changed his life forever. For days, he couldn't get the idea out of his mind. At only 12 years of age, Tim recognized that the kids he was hanging out with were not the ones he wanted influencing his future. So he went to his mom and dad and asked them to send him to private school. Four years at St. Paul's School set him on a path that led to a junior year abroad in Japan studying judo and Zen meditation; 4 years at Princeton University, where he became an all-American wrestler; a national kickboxing championship; and eventually starting his own company at the age of 23. Tim knew what every parent intuitively knows – that we become like the people we hang out with.

Why else are parents always telling their kids that they don't want them hanging out with "those kids"? It's because we know that kids (and adults!) become like the people they hang out with. That is why it is so important to spend time with the people you want to become like. If you want to be more successful, you have to start hanging out with more successful people.

There are lots of places to find successful people. Join a professional association. Attend your professional conferences. Join the chamber of commerce. Join the country club. Join the Young Presidents' Organization or the Young Entrepreneurs Organization. Volunteer for leadership positions. Join civic groups like Kiwanis, Optimists International, and Rotary International. Volunteer to serve with other leaders in your church, temple, or mosque. Attend lectures, symposia, courses, seminars, clinics, camps, and retreats taught by those who have already achieved what you want to achieve. Fly first class or business class whenever you can.

You Become Like the People You Spend the Most Time With

Pay any price to stay in the presence
of extraordinary people.

Mike Murdock – Author of *The Leadership Secrets of Jesus*

John Assaraf is a successful entrepreneur who has seemingly done it all – including traveling the world for a year in his twenties, owning and operating a franchising company whose annual real estate revenues topped $3 billion, and helping to build Internet virtual tour pioneer Bamboo.com (now IPEX) from a team of 6 people to a team of 1,500 in just over a year, netting millions in monthly sales and completing a successful initial public offering on the NASDAQ after just 9 months.

John was a street kid who had been entangled in the world of drugs and gangs. When he landed a job working in the gym at the Jewish community center across the street from his apartment in Montreal, his life was changed by the powerful principle that you become like the people you spend the most time with. In addition to earning $1.65 an hour, he received access to the men's health club. John recounts that he got his early education in business in the men's sauna. Every night after work, from 9:15 to 10 pm, you'd find him in the steamy hot room listening to successful businessmen tell their tales of success and failure.

Many of those successful men were immigrants who had come to Canada to stake their claim, and John was fascinated as much by their setbacks as by their successes. The stories of what went wrong with their businesses, families, and health gave him inspiration, because his own family was experiencing tremendous challenges and difficulties, and John learned that it was normal to have challenges – that other families also went through similar crises and still made it to the top.

These successful people taught John to never give up on his dreams. "No matter what the failure," they told him, "try another way; try going up, over, around, or through, but never give up. There's always a way." John also learned from these successful men that it makes no difference where you are born, what race or color you are, how old you are, or whether you come from a rich family or a poor family. Many of the men in that sauna spoke broken English; some were single and some were divorced; some were happily married and some were not; some were healthy and others were in terrible shape; some had college degrees and some didn't. Some hadn't even been to high school. For the first time, John realized that success is not reserved just for those born into well-to-do families without challenges and to whom every advantage has been given. He realized that no matter what the conditions of your life, you could build a life of success. He was in the presence of men from all walks of life who had done it and freely shared their wisdom and experience with him.

Every night John attended his own private business school – in a sauna in a Jewish community center. You, too, need to be surrounded with those who have done it; you need to be surrounded with people who have a positive attitude, a solution-oriented approach to life – people who know that they can accomplish whatever they set out to do.

Confidence is contagious. So is lack of confidence.

Vince Lombardi – Head coach of the Green Bay Packers who led them to six division titles, five NFL championships, and two Super Bowls (I and II)

Drop Out of the "Ain't It Awful" Club

There are two types of people – anchors and motors. You want to lose the anchors and get with the motors because the motors are going somewhere and they're having more fun. The anchors will just drag you down.

Wyland – World-renowned marine artist

When I was a first-year history teacher in a Chicago high school, I quickly stopped going into the teachers' lounge, which I soon dubbed the Ain't It Awful Club. Worse than the haze of cigarette smoke that constantly hung over the room was the cloud of emotional negativity. "Can you believe what they want us to do now?" "I got that Simmons kid again this year in math. He's a holy terror." "There is no way you can teach these kids. They are totally out of control." It was a constant stream of negative judgments, criticisms, blaming, and complaining. Not too long after, I discovered a group of dedicated teachers that hung out in the library and ate together at two tables in the teachers' lunchroom. They were positive and believed they could overcome and handle anything that was thrown at them. I implemented every new idea they shared with me, as well as a few more that I picked up from my weekend classes at the University of Chicago. As a result, I was selected by the students as teacher of the year in only my first year of teaching.

Be Selective

> I just do not hang around anybody that I don't want to be with. Period. For me, that's been a blessing, and I can stay positive. I hang around people who are happy, who are growing, who want to learn, who don't mind saying sorry or thank you ... and [are] having a fun time.
>
> **John Assaraf** – Author, *The Street Kid's Guide to Having It All*

I'd like you to do a valuable exercise that my mentor W. Clement Stone did with me. Make a list of everyone you spend time with on a regular basis – your family members, coworkers, neighbors, friends, people in your civic organization, fellow members of your religious group, and so on.

When you've completed your list, go back and put a minus sign (−) next to those people who are negative and toxic, and a plus sign (+) next to those who are positive and nurturing. As you make a decision about each person, you might find that a pattern will begin to form. Perhaps your entire workplace is filled with toxic personalities. Or perhaps it's your friends who naysay everything you do. Or maybe it's your family members who constantly put you down and undermine your self-esteem and self-confidence.

I want you to do the same thing that Mr. Stone told me to do. Stop spending time with those people with a minus sign next to their name. If that is impossible (and remember, nothing is impossible; it is always a choice), then severely decrease the amount of time you spend with them. You have to free yourself from the negative influence of others.

Think about it. I'm sure you know people who only have to walk into the room to totally drain you of energy. I refer to these people as psychic vampires. They literally suck the life energy right out of you. Stop spending time with them.

Are there people in your life who are always complaining and blaming others for their circumstances? Are there people who are always judging others, spreading negative gossip, and talking about how bad it is? Stop spending time with them as well.

Are there people in your life who, simply by calling you on the telephone, can bring tension, stress, and disorder to your day? Are there dream-stealers who tell you that your dreams are impossible and try to dissuade you from believing in and pursuing your goals? Do you have friends who constantly attempt to bring you back down to their level? If so, then it is time for some new friends!

Avoid Toxic People

Until you reach the point in your self-development where you no longer allow people to affect you with their negativity, you need to avoid toxic people at all costs. You're better off spending time alone than spending time with people who will hold you back with their victim mentality and their mediocre standards.

Make a conscious effort to surround yourself with positive, nourishing, and uplifting people – people who believe in you, encourage you to go after your dreams, and applaud your victories. Surround yourself with possibility thinkers, idealists, and visionaries.

Surround Yourself
with Successful People

One of the clients who hired me to teach these success principles to their salespeople is one of the leading manufacturers of optical lenses. As I mingled with the salespeople prior to the event, I asked each person I met if he or she knew who the top five salespeople in the company were. Most answered yes and quickly rattled off their names. That night I asked my audience of 300 people to raise their hands if they knew the names of the top five salespeople. Almost everyone raised a hand. I then asked them to raise their hands again if they had ever gone up to any of these five people and asked them to share their secrets of success. Not one hand went up. Think about it! Everyone knew who the most effective people in the company were, but because of an unfounded fear of rejection, nobody had ever asked these sales leaders to share their secrets with them.

If you are going to be successful, you have to start hanging out with the successful people. You need to ask them to share their success strategies with you. Then try them on and see if they fit for you. Experiment with doing what they do, reading what they read, thinking the way they think, and so on. If the new ways of thinking and behaving work, adopt them. If not, drop them, and keep looking and experimenting.

Principle 22

Clean Up Your Messes and Your Incompletes

If a cluttered desk is the sign of a cluttered mind,
what is the significance of a clean desk?

Laurence J. Peter – American educator and author

Take a look at the diagram above. It's called the Cycle of
Completion. Each of these steps – Decide, Plan, Start,
Continue, Finish, and Complete – is required to succeed at
anything, to get a desired result, to finish. Yet how many
of us never *complete*? We get all the way through the finishing stage – but leave one last thing undone.

Are there areas in your life where you've left uncom-
pleted projects or failed to get closure with people? When

you don't complete the past, you can't be free to fully embrace the present.

Failing to Complete Robs You of Valuable Attention Units

When you start a project or make an agreement or identify a change you need to make, it goes into your present memory bank and takes up what I call an attention unit. We can only pay attention to so many things at one time, and each promise, agreement, or item on your to-do list leaves fewer attention units to dedicate to completing present tasks and bringing new opportunities and abundance into your life.

So why don't people complete? Often, incompletes represent areas in our life where we're not clear – or where we have emotional and psychological blocks.

For instance, you might have a lot of requests, projects, tasks, and other things on your desk you really want to say no to – but you're afraid of being perceived as the bad guy. So you put off responding to avoid saying no. Meanwhile the sticky notes and stacks of paper pile up and distract you. There may also be circumstances in which you have to make decisions that are difficult or uncomfortable. So rather than struggle with the discomfort, you let the incompletes pile up.

Some incompletions come from simply not having

adequate systems, knowledge, or expertise for handling these tasks. Other incompletions pile up because of our bad work habits.

Get into Completion Consciousness

Continually ask yourself, *What does it take to actually get this task completed?* Then you can begin to consciously take that next step of filing completed documents, mailing in the forms required, or reporting back to your boss that the project has been completed. The truth is that 20 things *completed* have more power than 50 things half completed. One finished book, for instance, that can go out and influence the world is better than 13 books you're in the process of writing. Rather than starting 15 projects that end up incomplete and take up space in the house, you'd be better off if you had started just 3 and completed them.

The Four D's of Completion

One way to take care of to-do items is something we've all seen in time management courses: Do it, delegate it, delay it, or dump it. When you pick up a piece of paper, decide then and there whether you'll ever do anything with it. If not, dump it. If you can take care of it within 10 minutes, do it immediately. If you still want to take care of it your-self, but know it will take longer, delay it by filing it in a folder of things to do later. If you can't do it yourself or don't want to take the time, delegate it to someone you trust to accomplish the task. Be sure to have the person re-port back when he or she finishes the task so that you know it is complete.

Making Space for Something New

In addition to professional incompletes, most households are also groaning under the weight of too much clutter, too many papers, worn-out clothes, unused toys, forgot-ten personal effects, and obsolete, broken, and unneeded items. In the United States, the entire ministorage industry has sprung up to help homeowners and small businesses store what they can't fit in their homes and offices.

But do we really need all this stuff? Of course not.

One of the ways to free up attention units is to free your living and work environment from the mental burden of this clutter. When you clear out the old, you also make room for something new.

Take a look at your clothes closet, for instance. If you've got one of those where you can't put another thing into it – where you struggle to pull out a dress or shirt – that may be one reason why you don't have more new clothes. There's nowhere to put them. If you haven't worn something in 6 months and it's not a seasonal or a special-occasion item such as an evening gown or tuxedo, get rid of it.

If there's anything new that you want in your life, you've got to make room for it. I mean that psychologically as well as physically.

If you want a new man in your life, you've got to let go of (forgive and forget) the last one you stopped dating 5 years ago. Because if you don't, when a new man meets you, the unspoken message he picks up is "This woman's attached to somebody else. She hasn't let go."

My good friend Martin Rutte once told me that whenever he wants to bring in new business, he thoroughly cleans his office, home, car, and garage. Every time he does, he starts getting calls and letters from people who want to work with him. Others find that doing spring cleaning helps them gain new clarity on problems, challenges, opportunities, and relationships.

When we don't throw away clutter and items we no longer need, it's as if we don't trust our ability to manifest the necessary abundance in our lives to buy new ones. But incompletes like this keep that very abundance from showing up. We need to complete the past so that our present can show up more fully.

Twenty-Five Ways to Complete Before Moving Forward

How many things do you need to complete, dump, or delegate before you can move on and bring new activity, abundance, relationships, and excitement into your life? Use the checklist below to jog your thinking, make a list, and then write down how you'll complete each task.

Once you've made your list, choose four items and start completing them. Choose those that would immediately free up the most time, energy, or space for you – whether it's mental space or physical space.

At minimum, I encourage you to clean up one major incomplete every 3 months. If you want to really get the ball rolling, schedule a "completion weekend," and devote 2 full days to handling as many things on the following list as possible.

1. Former business activities
2. Promises not kept, not acknowledged, or not renegotiated
3. Unpaid debts or financial commitments (money owed to others or to you)
4. Closets overflowing with clothing never worn
5. A disorganized garage crowded with old discards
6. Haphazard or disorganized tax records
7. Checkbook not balanced or accounts that should be closed

8. "Junk drawers" full of unusable items
9. Missing or broken tools
10. An attic filled with unused items
11. A car trunk or backseat full of trash
12. Incomplete car maintenance
13. A disorganized basement filled with discarded items
14. Credenza packed with completed or unrealized projects
15. Filing left undone
16. Computer files not backed up or data needing to be converted for storage
17. Desk surface cluttered or disorganized
18. Family pictures never put into an album
19. Mending, ironing, or other piles of items to repair or discard
20. Deferred household maintenance
21. Personal relationships with unstated resentments or appreciations
22. People you need to forgive
23. Time not spent with people you've been meaning to spend time with
24. Incomplete projects or projects delivered without closure or feedback
25. Acknowledgments that need to be given or asked for

What's Irritating You?

Like incompletes, daily irritants are equally damaging to your success because they, too, take up attention units. Perhaps it's the missing button on your favorite suit that keeps you from wearing it to an important meeting or the torn screen on your patio door that lets in annoying insects. One of the best things you can do to move further and faster along your success path is to fix, replace, mend, or get rid of those daily irritants that annoy you and stay on your mind.

Talane Miedaner, the author of *Coach Yourself to Success*, recommends walking through every room of your house, your garage, and all around your property, jotting down those things that irritate, annoy, and bother you and then arranging to get each one handled. Of course, none of these may be urgent to your business or life-threatening to your family. But every time you notice them and wish they were different, they pull energy from you. They are subtly subtracting energy from your life instead of adding energy to your life.

Consider Hiring a Professional Organizer to Get You Started

The mission of the National Association of Professional Organizers (NAPO) is to help you declutter your life and build systems to ensure that things stay that way. You may need someone who has a dispassionate eye to look beyond your attachments, familiarity, and fears and be neutral in a way you can't. Plus, NAPO members are experts in how to make things efficient and easy. It is their profession.[1]

For about the cost of several business lunches, you can hire an organizer from your local area for a day of work. Additionally, you can hire people to clean your home, as well as handle all the little irritants, maintenance chores, and other tasks you either don't want to do or aren't skilled enough to do.

If your finances don't allow for a professional organizer, ask a friend to help. Hire a neighborhood teen or the stay-at-home mom down the street. You can also read one of the many good how-to books and tackle things yourself.[2] Just remember that you don't need to get it done all at once. Choose one each month. Just as cleaning up your incompletes is important to your successful future, there is literally no excuse for enduring the disorganization in your life.

Principle 23

Develop Four New Success Habits a Year

The individual who wants to reach the top in business must appreciate the might and force of habit. He must be quick to break those habits that can break him – and hasten to adopt those practices that will become the habits that help him achieve the success he desires.

J. Paul Getty – Founder of Getty Oil Company, philanthropist, and, by the late 1950s, widely regarded as the richest man in the world

Psychologists tell us that up to 90% of our behavior is habitual. 90%! From the time you get up in the morning until the time you retire at night, there are hundreds of things you do the same way every day. These include the way you shower, dress, eat breakfast, read the newspaper, brush your teeth, drive to work, organize your desk, shop at the supermarket, and clean your house. Over the years, you have developed a set of firmly entrenched habits that determine how well every area of your life works, from your job and your income to your health and your relationships.

The good news is that habits help free up your mind while your body is on automatic. This allows you to plan your day while you are in the shower and talk to your fellow passengers while you are driving your car. The bad news is that you can become locked into unconscious self-defeating behavior patterns that inhibit your growth and limit your success.

Whatever habits you currently have established are producing your current level of results. More than likely, if you want to create higher levels of success, you are going to need to drop some of your habits (not returning phone calls, staying up too late watching television, making sarcastic comments, eating fast food every day, smoking, being late for appointments, spending more than you earn) and replace them with more productive habits (returning phone calls within 24 hours, getting 8 hours of sleep each day, reading for an hour a day, exercising four times a week, eating healthy food, being on time, and saving 10% of your income).

Good or Bad, Habits Always Deliver Results

Success is a matter of understanding and religiously practicing specific, simple habits that always lead to success.

Robert J. Ringer – Author of *Million Dollar Habits*

Your habits determine your outcomes. Successful people don't just drift to the top. Getting there requires focused action, personal discipline, and lots of energy every day to make things happen. The habits you develop from this day forward will ultimately determine how your future unfolds.

One of the problems for people with poor habits is that the results of their bad habits usually don't show up until much later in life. When you develop a chronic bad habit, life will eventually give you consequences. You may not like the consequences, but life will still deliver them. The fact is, if you keep on doing things a certain way, you will always get a predictable result. Negative habits breed negative consequences. Positive habits create positive consequences.

Take Action to Develop Better Habits Now

There are two action steps for changing your habits: The *first step* is to make a list of all the habits that keep you unproductive or that might negatively impact your future. Ask others to help you objectively identify what they believe are your limiting habits. Look for patterns. Also review the list of the most common unsuccessful habits below:

- Procrastinating
- Paying bills at the last minute
- Not delivering on promised documents and services in a timely way
- Letting receivables get overdue
- Arriving late for meetings and appointments
- Forgetting someone's name within seconds of being introduced
- Talking over others' comments, instead of listening
- Answering the telephone during family time or spouse time
- Handling the mail more than once
- Working late
- Choosing work over time with your children
- Having fast-food meals more than 2 days a week

Once you have identified your negative habits, the *second*

step is to choose a better, more productive success habit and develop systems that will help support them.

For example, if your goal is to get to the gym every morning, one system you might put in place is to go to bed 1 hour earlier and set your alarm ahead. If you're in sales, you might develop a checklist of activities so that all prospects receive the same series of communications.

Maybe you want to get in the habit of completing your work by close of business Friday, so you're free to spend weekends with your spouse and children. That's an excellent habit, *but what specifically will you do to adopt that new habit?* What activities will you engage in? How will you stay motivated? Will you develop a checklist of what must be accomplished by Friday afternoon to keep you on track? Will you spend less time chatting with coworkers at the water cooler? E-mail people their promised documents as you are talking on the phone with them? Take shorter lunches?

What Could You Achieve if You Took on Four New Habits a Year?

If you use these strategies to develop just four new habits a year, 5 years from now you'll have 20 new success habits that could bring you all the money you want, the wonderful loving relationships you desire, a healthier, more energized body, plus all sorts of new opportunities.

Start by listing four new habits you would like to establish in the next year. Work on one new habit every quarter. If you work diligently on building one new habit every 13 weeks, you won't overwhelm yourself with an unrealistic list of New Year's resolutions ... and research now shows that if you repeat a behavior for 13 weeks – whether it is meditating for 20 minutes a day, flossing your teeth, reviewing your goals, or writing thank-you letters to your clients – it will be yours for life. By systematically adding one behavior at a time, you can dramatically improve your overall lifestyle.

Here are a couple of hints for making sure you follow through on your commitment to your new habit. Put up signs to remind you to follow through on the new behavior. When I learned that even a little dehydration can decrease your mental acuity by as much as 30%, I decided to develop the habit that all of the health practitioners had been advising – drink ten 8-ounce glasses of water a day. I put signs that said "Drink water!" on my phone, my office door, my bathroom mirror, and my kitchen refrigerator. I also had my secretary remind me every hour. Another powerful technique is to partner up with someone, keep score, and hold each other accountable. Check in with each other at least once a week to make sure you are staying on track.

Principle 24

Stay Focused on Your Core Genius

Success follows doing what you want to do.
There is no other way to be successful.

Malcolm S. Forbes – Publisher of *Forbes* magazine

I believe you have inside you a core genius – some one thing that you love to do and do so well that you hardly feel like charging people for it. It's effortless for you and a whole lot of fun. And if you could make money doing it, you'd make it your lifetime's work.

Successful people believe this, too. That's why they put their core genius first. They focus on it – and delegate everything else to other people on their team.

Compare that to the other people in the world who go through life doing everything, even those tasks they're bad at or that could be done more cheaply, better, and faster by someone else. They can't find the time to focus on their core genius because they fail to delegate even the most menial of tasks.

When you delegate the grunt work – the things you hate doing or those tasks that are so painful, you end up putting them off – you get to concentrate on what you love to do. You free up your time so that you can be more productive. And you get to enjoy life more.

So why is delegating routine tasks and unwanted projects so difficult for most people?

Surprisingly, most people are afraid of looking wasteful or being judged as being above everyone else. They are afraid to give up control or reluctant to spend the money to pay for help. Deep down, most people simply don't want to let go.

Others – potentially you – have simply fallen into the *habit* of doing everything themselves. "It's too time-consuming to explain it to someone," you say. "I can do it more quickly and better myself anyway." But can you?

Delegate Completely

If you're a professional earning $75 per hour and you pay a neighborhood kid $10 an hour to cut the grass, you save the effort of doing it yourself on the weekend and gain 1 extra hour when you could profit by $65. Of course, though 1 hour doesn't seem like much, multiply that by at least 20 weekends in the spring and summer and you discover you've gained 20 hours a year at $65 per hour – or an extra $1,300 in potential earnings.

Similarly, if you're a real estate agent, you need to list houses, gather information for the multiple listings, attend open houses, do showings, put keys in lockboxes, write offers, and make appointments. And if you're lucky, you eventually get to close a deal.

But let's say that you're the best closer in the area.

Why would you want to waste your time writing listings, doing lead generation, placing lockboxes, and making videos of the property when you could have a staff of colleagues and assistants doing all that, thus freeing you up to do more closing? Instead of doing just one deal a week, you could be doing three deals because you had delegated what you're less good at.

One of the strategies I use and teach is complete delegation. It simply means that you delegate a task once and completely – rather than delegating it each time it needs to be done.

When I hired the gardener for my Santa Barbara estate, I said, "I want my grounds to look as close as possible to the grounds at the Four Seasons Biltmore in Montecito using the budget I'm providing you." When I go to the Four Seasons, I don't have to check whether the trees need to be trimmed or the automatic sprinklers are working. Someone else is in charge of that. Well, I want the same luxury at my home. "With that as our operating principle," I said, "here's the budget. Take charge of the grounds. If I'm ever not happy, I'll let you know. If I'm not happy a second time, I'll find someone else. Does that feel like a workable agreement?"

My landscaper was, in fact, very excited. He knew he wouldn't be micromanaged, and I knew I wouldn't have to worry about it again – and I don't. See what I mean? Complete delegation.

When my niece came to stay with us one year while

she attended the local community college, we made another complete delegation – the grocery shopping. We told her she could have unlimited use of our van if she would buy the groceries every week. We provided her with a list of staples that we always want in the house (eggs, butter, milk, ketchup, and so on), and her job was to check every week and replace anything that was running low. In addition, my wife planned meals and let her know which items she wanted for the main courses (fish, chicken, broccoli, avocadoes, and so on). The task was delegated once and saved us hundreds of hours that year that could be devoted to writing, exercise, family time, and recreation.

Become a Con Artist Doing What You Love to Do

> The biggest mistake people make in life is not trying to make a living at doing what they most enjoy.
>
> Malcolm S. Forbes

Strategic Coach Dan Sullivan once stated that all entrepreneurs are really con artists. They get other people to pay them to practice getting better at what they love to do.[1]

Think about it.

Tiger Woods loves to play golf. People pay him big money to play golf. Every time he plays, he learns more about playing better. He gets to practice and hang out with other golfers, all the while getting paid for it.

Anthony Robbins is a speaker and a trainer. He loves speaking and training. He has arranged his life so that people are constantly paying him large sums of money to do what he loves to do.

Or consider baseball great Sammy Sosa of the Chicago Cubs. It takes him about 1 second to hit a home run – as long as it takes for the ball to meet the bat. He earns $10,625,000 for about 70 seconds of batting time per year, so he has gotten really good at making the bat meet the ball. That's where he makes his money. That's where he puts all his time – practicing and getting ready for the bat to meet the ball. He has found his core genius and devotes the majority of his waking hours to perfecting his genius.

Of course, most of us are not on par with Tiger Woods, Tony Robbins, or Sammy Sosa, but the fact is that we could learn a lot from their level of focus.

Many salespeople, for example, spend more time on account administration than they do on the phone making sales, when they *could* hire a part-time administrator (or share the cost with another salesperson) to do this time-consuming detail work.

Most female executives spend too much time running their household, when they could easily and inexpensively delegate this task to a cleaning service or part-time mother's helper, freeing themselves to focus on their career or spend more time with their family.

Even most entrepreneurs spend less than 30% of their time focusing on their core genius and unique abilities. In fact, by the time they've launched a business, it often seems entrepreneurs are doing everything *but* the one thing they went into business for in the first place.

Don't let this be your fate. Identify your core genius, then delegate completely to free up more time to focus on what you love to do.

Do What You Love – The Money Will Follow

> Starting out to make money is the greatest mistake in life. Do what you feel you have a flair for doing, and if you are good enough at it, the money will come.
>
> **Greer Garson** – Winner of the 1943 Academy Award for best actress

Diana von Welanetz Wentworth is someone who has always focused on her core genius while following her heart and has been wildly successful as a result. Her greatest pleasure was always to be cooking something and gathering people around the table to share at a deep level over food. She was always reaching for a deeper connection, what she calls "a sense of celebration at the table." So she started her career writing books about how to give a party and do everything ahead of time so you can actually be present and connect more deeply with the people you invite.

Then in May 1985, she went on a trip to the Soviet Union with a group of leaders in the human potential movement, where she noticed that, for the most part, they were all loners. Even though they were quite well known for their books and their impact in the world, they didn't know each other. When she returned, she realized that her life purpose had always been more about connection than food. She had just used food as a catalyst.

That realization led her to create the Inside Edge, an organization that hosted weekly breakfast meetings in Beverly Hills, Orange County, and San Diego, California, where nationally recognized people of vision came together to share their knowledge and wisdom on human potential, spirituality, consciousness, and world peace. Speakers included people such as Mark Victor Hansen and me, motivational expert Anthony Robbins, management consultant Ken Blanchard, actor Dennis Weaver, counselor the Reverend Leo Booth, and authors Susan Jeffers and Dan Millman. In addition to listening to an inspirational speaker, participants would network, encourage each other to dream bigger, and support each other's projects. Eighteen years later, the Orange County chapter still continues to meet every week.[2]

Diana has gone on to write and coauthor numerous books, including *The Chicken Soup for the Soul Cookbook*, once again integrating her love of food with her love of people sharing their ideas, wisdom, and stories.

Start Now!
… Just Do It!

> Many people die with their music still in them. Why is this so? Too often it is because they are always getting ready to live. Before they know it, time runs out.
>
> **Oliver Wendell Holmes** – Former U.S. Supreme Court Justice

There is no perfect time to start. If you are into astrology and you want to contact your astrologer about an auspicious date to get married, open your store, launch a new product line, or begin a concert tour, okay – that's fine. I can understand that. But for everything else, the best strategy is just to jump in and get started. Don't keep putting things off waiting for 12 doves to fly over your house in the sign of a cross before you begin. Just start.

You want to be a public speaker? Fine. Schedule a free talk for a local service club, school, or church group. Just having a date will put the pressure on you to start researching and writing your speech. If that's too big of a stretch, then join Toastmasters or take a speech class.

You want to be in the restaurant business? Go get a job in a restaurant and start learning the business. You want to be a chef? Great! Enroll in a cooking school. Take action and get started – today! You do not have to know every-thing to get going. Just get into the game. You will learn by doing.

First you jump off the cliff and
you build wings on the way down.

Ray Bradbury – Prolific American author of science fiction and fantasy

Don't get me wrong here. I am a big proponent of educa-tion, training, and skill building. If you need more training, then go and get it. Sign up for that class or that seminar now. You may need a coach or a mentor to get where you want to go. If so, then go get one. If you're afraid, so what? Feel the fear and do it anyway. The key is to just get start-ed. Quit waiting until you are *perfectly* ready. You never will be.

I started out my career as a history teacher in a Chicago high school. I was far from the perfect teacher on my first day of teaching school. I had a lot to learn about class-room control, effective discipline, how to avoid getting conned by a slick student, how to confront manipulative behavior, and how to motivate an unmotivated student. But I had to start anyway. And it was in the process of teaching that I learned all of those other things.

Most of life is on-the-job training. Some of the most im-portant things can only be learned in the process of doing them. You do something and you get feedback – about what works and what doesn't. If you don't do anything for fear of doing it wrong, poorly, or badly, you never get any feedback, and therefore you never get to improve.

When I started my first business, a retreat and conference center in Amherst, Massachusetts, called the New England Center for Personal and Organizational Development, I went to a local bank to get a loan. The first bank I went to told me I needed to have a business plan. I didn't know what that was, but I went and bought a book on how to write a business plan. I wrote one up and took it to the bank. They told me there were a bunch of holes in my plan. I asked what they were, and they told me. I went back and rewrote the plan, filling in the areas I had left out or that were unclear or unconvincing. I then went back to the bank. They said the plan was good, but they wanted to pass. I asked them who might be willing to fund the plan. They gave me the names of several bankers in the area they thought might respond favorably. Again I went off to the bank. Each one gave us more feedback until I had honed the plan and my presentation to the point where I did finally obtain the $20,000 loan that we needed.

When Mark Victor Hansen and I first released *Chicken Soup for the Soul*®, I thought it would be a good idea to sell the book in bulk quantity to some of the larger network marketing companies, thinking they could give them or resell them to their sales force to motivate them to believe in their dreams, take more risks, and therefore achieve greater success in selling. I got a list of all the companies that belonged to the Direct Marketing Association, and I started cold-calling the sales directors of the larger companies. Sometimes I couldn't get the sales director to take my call. Other times I was told, "We're not interested." Several times I was actually hung up on! But eventually, after getting better at getting through to the right decision maker and properly discussing the book's potential benefits, I made several significant sales. A few of the companies liked the book so much they later hired me to speak at their national conventions.

Was I a little scared making cold calls? Yes. Did I know what I was doing when I started? No. I had never tried to sell mass quantities of books to anyone before. I had to learn as I went. But the most important point is that I just got started. I got into communication with the people I wanted to serve; found out what their dreams, aspirations, and goals were; and explored how our book might help them in achieving their objectives. Everything unfolded because I was willing to take a risk and jump into the ring.

You, too, have to begin – from wherever you are – to start taking the actions that will get you to where you want to be.

How to get started

A journey of 1,000 miles must begin with one step.

Ancient Chinese proverb

The key to success is to take what you have learned (or re-learned) in this book and put it into action. You can't do everything at once, but you can begin. There are 25 principles in this book. If you're not careful, that could feel a bit overwhelming to you. So here is all you have to do:

Go back to the beginning and start working through each principle one at a time, in the order they are presented – take 100% responsibility for your life and your success, clarify your life purpose, decide what you want, set specific and measurable goals for all the parts of your personal vision, break them down into specific action steps you can take, create affirmations for each one of your goals, and begin the practice of visualizing your completed goals every day.

Then begin *taking action* on your most important goals *every day*. Ask for whatever you need with no fear of rejection, ask for and respond to feedback, commit to never-ending improvement, and persist in the face of whatever obstacles may come up. Now you're up and running toward the completion of your major goals.

Next, to build and maintain momentum, create a program for cleaning up your incompletes, pick a habit to work on developing for the next quarter, commit to reading one of the books in "Suggested Reading and Additional Resources for Success" (and then another and another), and purchase a motivational audio program to listen to in your car or when you are exercising.

You can't do everything at once. But if you keep adding a little progress every day, over time you will have built a whole new set of habits and self-disciplines. Remember, anything valuable takes time. There are no overnight successes. It took me years to learn and implement all of the principles in this book. I have mastered some and am still working on mastering others.

Though it will take you some time, it shouldn't have to take you as long as it took me. I had to discover all of these principles on my own over a period of many years and from many different sources. I am passing them all on to you in one package. Take advantage of my having gone before and blazed a trail for you. Everything you need is here to take you to the next level.

Granted, ...ere are things you'll need to learn that are unique to your specific situation, profession, career, and goals that are not covered in this book, but the fundamental principles needed to succeed in *any* venture are contained here. Make the commitment to start now and get on with using them to create the life of your dreams.

Precessional Effects

Scientist, inventor, and philosopher Buckminster Fuller talked about the precessional effects that issue from just getting started in the service of humanity. Fuller explained precession by pointing out that the honeybee's seemingly primary objective is to obtain nectar to make honey, but while going after the nectar, the honeybee is unwittingly involved in a much bigger purpose. As it flies from flower to flower in search of more nectar, it picks up pollen on its wings and thus ends up cross-pollinating all the rooted botanicals in the world. It's an unintended byproduct of the bee's nectar-seeking activity. Think of yourself as a speedboat moving through the water. To the sides of you and behind you is a wake of activity caused by the sheer force of your forward motion. Life is like that, too. As long as you are actively in motion in the pursuit of your goals, you will create precessional effects that will turn out to be far more important than you initially were capable of understanding or intending. You just begin, and the path of opportunities just keeps unfolding in front of and to the side of you.

None of the wealthy and successful people I know (both my closest friends and the more than 70 people I interviewed for this book) could have possibly planned or predicted the exact sequence of events that unfolded over the course of their lives. They all started with a dream and a plan, but once they started, things unfolded in unexpected ways.

Look at my own example. Mark Victor Hansen and I never predicted that *Chicken Soup for the Soul®*, the title of our first book, would evolve into a brand name and would become a household phrase in North America and numerous other countries around the globe. Nor could we have ever predicted that we would have a line of Chicken Soup for the Pet Lover's Soul™ dog and cat foods, a line of greeting cards, a television show, a syndicated column, or a syndicated radio show. All of these things just evolved out of our initial commitment to write a book and be of service.

When Dave Liniger decided to leave the biggest real estate agency in Denver and start his own agency, he had no idea that 30 years later his company, RE/MAX, would become the largest real estate agency in the United States, a billion-dollar business with 92,000 agents in 50 countries around the world.

When Donald Trump built his first building, he wasn't aware that he would eventually own casinos, golf courses, a resort, the Miss USA contest, and the number-one reality show on American television. He just knew he wanted to build magnificent buildings. The rest unfolded along the way.

Carl Tarcher started with a rolling hot dog stand in downtown Los Angeles. As he made a little money, he bought another one and then another one until he could buy a real restaurant. That one restaurant evolved into Carl's Junior.

When Paul Orfalea started out with a single copy shop

to serve local college students, little did he know it would evolve into a chain of over 1,800 Kinko's stores and net him $116 million when he later sold it.

All of these people may have had a set of goals and a detailed plan as best as they could conceive it at the time, but each new success opened up new unforeseen possibilities. If you just aim in the direction you want to go, start, and keep moving forward, all kinds of unforeseen opportunities will grow out of that forward motion.

Meeting Vin Di Bona

When the first *Chicken Soup for the Soul*® book hit the best seller lists, our publisher asked us if we would start working on a sequel. He also asked us if we would be willing to create a cookbook of chicken soup recipes. Though that seemed like too limiting a focus for a book – how many chicken soup recipes can one person use? – the idea of creating a cookbook interested us. One of our close friends, Diana von Welanetz Wentworth, is an award-winning cookbook author who had already dedicated her life to making a difference in the world. The idea for a book of stories written by famous people, celebrated cookbook authors, chefs, and restaurateurs, accompanied by a recipe that tied into the story, did intrigue us. And so we asked Diana to collaborate with us on such a book. Together we gathered moving stories that centered on a meaningful experience with food accompanied with the recipe for that food.

The best part of the project was that Diana would prepare each recipe to make sure that it actually worked and tasted good. Then every couple of weeks, Mark and I would go to Diana's house and eat the results as we selected which of the hundreds of stories and recipes we would include in the book. (I don't remember losing any weight during that project!)

A year later, Mark and I began thinking all the stories we had been collecting would make good material for a television show. Other than being interviewed on a lot of talk shows and news programs to promote our books, Mark and I had no experience in the world of television. We didn't know any producers, directors, or programming executives at the networks. But we began to get the sense that television was a next step we should be exploring. Once we added a *Chicken Soup for the Soul®* television show to our goal list and started affirming and visualizing *Chicken Soup* on TV, it wasn't more than a couple of weeks before Diana called us and said, "You know, I've been thinking that I should introduce you to Vin Di Bona. He's the producer of America's *Funniest Home Videos*. He used to produce a cooking show that Paul and I did, and I think he might be interested in doing something on television with *Chicken Soup for the Soul®*."

Sure enough, through Diana's connection, we secured a meeting with Vin Di Bona and his company's vice president, Lloyd Weintraub. It turned out Lloyd was a big fan of *Chicken Soup*. He took over the meeting and totally sold Vin on the idea. A year later, we were in production with a series of 16 shows that aired on PAX TV and later on ABC, with such actors as Jack Lemmon, Ernest Borgnine, Martin Sheen, Stephanie Zimbalist, Teri Garr, Rod Steiger, and Charles Durning starring in each week's episodes.

Once you start moving and producing results, all manner of things begin to happen that will take you further and faster than you ever imagined.

An Olympic Dream Turns into a Professional Speaking Career

When Ruben Gonzalez finally realized his dream of competing in the winter Olympics for the third time, he returned home to Texas, where his 11-year-old neighbor reminded him of his promise to be his show-and-tell story at the local elementary school. After Ruben regaled Will's fifth-grade class with the tales of his struggles to achieve his Olympic dream, Will's teacher asked Ruben if he would be willing to address an assembly of the whole school. So Ruben stayed for another hour and talked to all 200 kids.

At the end of his talk, several teachers told him that they often hired speakers to come speak to the kids, and he was easily better than anyone they had previously hired. They told him that he had a natural gift as a speaker. Encouraged by this feedback, Ruben began calling up other schools in the Houston area, and soon had so many bookings that he quit his job as a copier salesman.

Everything went well until June, when to Ruben's surprise school let out for the summer and there were no more speaking engagements until the fall. Spurred on by the need to feed himself and his wife, Ruben began calling up local businesses. Little by little, he established a toehold in the corporate world around Dallas and, as word grew about his incredibly motivational talks, Ruben's career took off. Just under 2 years later, Ruben made as much money in the first 2 months of the year as he had made all year in his previous job as a copier salesman.

Placing thirty-fifth in the world in luge, a sport most people have never even heard of, was a step toward a career as a world-class speaker, but it was not something he was planning when he was plummeting down the ice track at 90 miles an hour at the U.S. Olympic Training Center in Lake Placid, New York. It was one of those precessional effects that Buckminster Fuller was talking about.

Go Get Started!

I have done my best to give you the principles and the tools you need to go and make all of your dreams come true. They have worked for me and for countless others, and they can work for you as well. But this is where the information, motivation, and inspiration stop, and the perspiration (provided by you) begins. You and you alone are responsible for taking the actions to create the life of your dreams. Nobody else can do it for you.

You have all of the talent and the resources you need to start right now and eventually create anything you want. I know you can do it. You know you can do it … so go out there and do it! It's a lot of fun as well as a lot of hard work. So remember to enjoy the journey!

Everyone who got to where they are
had to begin where they were.

Richard Paul Evans – Best-selling author of *The Christmas Box*

Notes

Principle 2

1. Robert Allen, coauthor of *The One Minute Millionaire*.
2. D.C. Cordova, cofounder of the Excellerated Business School.
3. Anthony Robbins, author of *Personal Power* and *Get the Edge*, entrepreneur, and philanthropist.
4. Monty Roberts, author of *The Man Who Listens to Horses*.
5. Mark Victor Hansen, coauthor of the *Chicken Soup for the Soul*® series.
6. T. Harv Eker, CEO of Peak Potentials and creator of the "Millionaire Mind" seminar.
7. There are many ways to approach defining your purpose. I learned this version of the life purpose exercise from Arnold M. Patent, spiritual coach and author of *You Can Have It All*. His most recent book is *The Journey*. You can visit his Web site at www.arnoldpatent.com.

Principle 3

1. To learn more about Monty and his work, go to www.montyroberts.com or read one of his books: *The Man Who Listens to Horses, Shy Boy, Horse Sense for People*, and *From My Hands to Yours*.

Principle 4

1. Adapted from "Placebos Prove So Powerful Even Experts Are Surprised: New Studies Explore the Brain's Triumph Over Reality" by Sandra Blakeslee. *New York Times*, October 13, 1998, section F, page 1.

Principle 5

1. From "Some Billionaires Choose School of Hard Knocks," June 29, 2000; Forbes.com, 2003 Forbes 400 Richest People in America. Statistics were revised based on the 2003 edition of the Forbes 400 Richest People in America.

Principle 8

1. For the best primer on mind mapping, see *The Mind Map Book* by Tony Buzan and Barry Buzan (London: BBC Books, 1993).
2. See *The Seven Spiritual Laws of Success: A Practical Guide to the Fulfillment of Your Dreams*, by Deepak

Chopra (San Rafael, Calif.: Amber-Allen, 1995); *The Spontaneous Fulfillment of All Desire: Harnessing the Infinite Power of Coincidence,* by Deepak Chopra (New York: Harmony Books, 2003); *The Power of Intention: Learning to Co-Create Your World Your Way,* by Wayne W. Dyer (Carlsbad, Calif.: Hay House, 2004); and *The 11th Element: The Key to Unlocking Your Master Blueprint for Wealth and Success,* by Robert Scheinfeld (Hoboken, N.J.: John Wiley & Sons, 2003).

Principle 9

1. Contact information for all of the books, seminars, and coaching programs mentioned throughout these pages can be found in "Suggested Reading and Additional Resources," starting on page 311. You can also access an updated and ever-expanding list of these kinds of resources at www.thesuccessprinciples.com.

Principle 10

1. From an interview in *Movieline,* July 1994.

Principle 12

1. *Not Your Mother's Midlife: A Ten-Step Guide to Fearless Aging,* by Nancy Alspaugh and Marilyn Kentz. Kansas City, Mo.: Andrews McMeel Universal, 2003, pages 180–181.

Principle 14

1. Ron Nielsen, Tim Piering, and I have used this same technique to create a new program to help fearful flyers overcome their fear of flying. For more information or to purchase a copy of *Chicken Soup for the Soul's Fearless FlightKit*™ for yourself or a friend, go online to www.fearless-flight.com.

2. If you have a phobia that is holding you back, visit Roger Callahan's Web site at www.tftrx.com or call 800-359-2873 and order the *Five-Minute Phobia Cure* videotape or schedule a phone session with Dr. Callahan. You can also go to any Internet search engine, type in "five-minute phobia cure" or "Thought Field Therapy," and look for a practitioner near you.

3. If you're interested in real estate investing, you can check out Robert's latest book, *Nothing Down for the 2000s: Dynamic New Wealth Strategies in Real Estate* (New York: Simon & Schuster, 2004).

4. *The Challenge*, by Robert Allen (New York: Simon & Schuster, 1987).

Principle 15

1. "Trash Talker," *Smithsonian*, April 2003, pages 116–117.

2. For more information on the Mississippi River Beautification and Restoration Project or how to participate in Adopt a Mississippi River Mile, you can visit Chad's Web site at www.livinglandsandwaters.org, call 309-

496-9848, or write Living Lands & Waters, 17615 Route 84 N., Great River Road, East Moline, IL 61244.

Principle 19

1. See www.xmradio.com for more information. Stock price is as of June 1, 2004.
2. Adapted from *David Frost's Book of Millionaires, Multimillionaires, and Really Rich People*, by David Frost (New York: Random House, 1984).

Principle 22

1. You can find organizers in your area by visiting the NAPO Web site and www.napo.net and clicking on "Find an Organizer." The following Web sites also help you locate professional organizers near you: www.organizersincanada.com and www.organizerswebring.com, which includes listings for seven countries. Martha Ringer is the productivity coach who has helped me organize my desk and my work flow. In 2 days' time, my office looked like a brand-new place, and my work flow is now clean and efficient. You can find her at www.martharinger.com.
2. Some of the best are
   – *Getting Organized*, by Stephanie Winston (New York: Bantam Books, 1978).
   – *Organizing from the Inside Out* (second edition), by Julie Morgenstern (New York: Henry Holt, 2004).

– *Organizing from the Inside Out for Teens*, by Julie Morgenstern and Jessi Morgenstern-Colón (New York: Henry Holt, 2002).

– *How to Be Organized in Spite of Yourself* (revised edition), by Sunny Schlenger and Roberta Roesch (New York: Signet Books, 1999).

– *Let Go of Clutter*, by Harriet Schecter (New York: McGraw-Hill, 2001).

Principle 24

1. I am grateful to Dan Sullivan for many of the ideas in this chapter. You can learn more about his breakthrough coaching ideas at www.strategiccoach.com.
2. Go to www.insideedge.org for more information on the Inside Edge.

Suggested Reading and Additional Resources

You are the same today as you'll be in five years
except for two things, the books you read
and the people you meet.

Charlie "Tremendous" Jones –
Member of the National Speakers Hall of Fame

I recommend that you read for an hour a day. That should add up to one or two books a week. I suggest you read through the list below and see which books jump out at you and start with those. Follow your interests, and you'll find that each book you read will lead you to other books.

There are also audio programs I suggest you listen to and training programs I encourage you to attend. For a more extensive and continually updated list of books, audio programs, and trainings in all of these areas, go to www.thesuccessprinciples.com.

The Science of Success

The Power of Focus: How to Hit Your Business, Personal and Financial Targets with Absolute Certainty, by Jack

Canfield, Mark Victor Hansen, and Les Hewitt. Deerfield Beach, Fla.: Health Communications, 2000.

The Aladdin Factor: How to Ask for and Get Anything You Want in Life, by Jack Canfield and Mark Victor Hansen. New York: Berkley, 1995.

The Art of Possibility: Transforming Personal and Professional Life, by Rosamund Stone Zander and Benjamin Zander. New York, Penguin, 2000.

The DNA of Success: Know What You Want ... To Get What You Want, by Jack M. Zufelt. New York: Regan Books, 2002.

The Science of Success: How to Attract Prosperity and Create Life Balance Through Proven Principles, by James A. Ray. La Jolla, Calif.: SunArk Press, 1999.

The Success System That Never Fails, by W. Clement Stone. Englewood Cliffs, N.J.: Prentice-Hall, 1962.

Success Through a Positive Mental Attitude, by Napoleon Hill and W. Clement Stone. Englewood Cliffs, N.J.: Prentice-Hall, 1977.

Think and Grow Rich, by Napoleon Hill. New York: Fawcett Crest, 1960.

Napoleon Hill's Keys to Success: The 17 Principles of Personal Achievement, edited by Matthew Sartwell. New York: Plume, 1997.

Think and Grow Rich: A Black Choice, by Dennis P. Kimbro, Ph.D. New York: Ballantine, 1997.

What Makes the Great Great: Strategies for Extraordinary Achievement, by Dennis P. Kimbrow, Ph.D. New York: Doubleday, 1997.

The 7 Habits of Highly Effective People, by Stephen R. Covey. New York: Fireside, 1989.

The 100 Absolutely Unbreakable Laws of Business Success, by Brian Tracy. San Francisco: Berret-Koehler, 2000.

Play to Win: Choosing Growth Over Fear in Work and Life, by Larry Wilson and Hersch Wilson. Austin, Tex.: Bard Press, 1998.

Master Success: Create a Life of Purpose, Passion, Peace and Prosperity, by Bill Fitzpatrick. Natick, Mass.: American Success Institute, 2000.

The Traits of Champions: The Secrets to Championship Performance in Business, Golf, and Life, by Andrew Wood and Brian Tracy. Provo, Utah: Executive Excellence Publishing, 2000.

The Great Crossover: Personal Confidence in the Age of the Microchip, by Dan Sullivan, Babs Smith, and Michel Néray. Chicago and Toronto: The Strategic Coach, 1994.

Extreme Success, by Richard Fettke. New York: Fireside, 2002.

The Power of Positive Habits, by Dan Robey. Miami: Abritt Publishing Group, 2003.

Unlimited Power, by Anthony Robbins. New York: Simon & Schuster, 1986.

The Official Guide to Success, by Tom Hopkins. Scottsdale, Ariz.: Champion Press, 1982.

Create Your Own Future, by Brian Tracy. New York: John Wiley & Sons, 2002.

The Street Kid's Guide to Having It All, by John Assaraf. San Diego: The Street Kid, LLC, 2003.

Peak Performance: Mental Training Techniques of the World's Greatest Athletes, by Charles A. Garfield, with Hal Z. Bennett. Los Angeles: Jeremy P. Tarcher, 1984.

Peak Performers: The New Heroes of American Business, by Charles Garfield. New York: William Morrow, 1986.

How to Use What You've Got to Get What You Want, by Marilyn Tam. San Diego: Jodere, 2003.

You Were Born Rich, by Bob Proctor. Willowdale, Ontario, Canada: McCrary Publishing, 1984.

The Magic of Believing, by Claude M. Bristol. New York: Simon & Schuster, 1991.

The Magic of Thinking Big, by David Schwartz. New York: Fireside, 1987.

Work Less, Make More, by Jennifer White. New York: John Wiley & Sons, 1998.

Ask and It Is Given: Learning to Manifest Your Desires, by Esther and Jerry Hicks. Carlsbad, Calif.: Hay House, 2004.

50 Success Classics, by Tom Butler-Bowdon. Yarmouth, Maine: Nicholas Brealey Publishing, 2004.

See You at the Top (2nd revision), by Zig Ziglar. New York: Pelican, 2000.

Entrepreneurial Success

All You Can Do Is All You Can Do But All You Can Do Is Enough!, by A. L. Williams. New York: Ivy Books, 1988.

The E-Myth Revisited: Why Most Small Businesses Don't Work and What to Do About It, by Michael Gerber. New York: HarperBusiness, 1995.

E-Myth Mastery: The Seven Essential Disciplines for Building a World Class Company, by Michael Gerber. New York: HarperBusiness, 2004.

Mastering the Rockefeller Habits, by Verne Harnish. New York: Select Books, 2002.

1001 Ways to Reward Employees, by Bob Nelson. New York: Workman Publishing, 1994.

The One Minute Manager, by Kenneth Blanchard and Spencer Johnson. New York: Berkley Books, 1983.

Start Small, Finish Big: Fifteen Key Lessons to Start—and Run—Your Own Successful Business, by Fred DeLuca with John B. Hayes. New York: Warner Books, 2000.

Corporate Success

Built to Last: The Successful Habits of Visionary Companies, by Jim Collins and Jerry I. Porras. New York: HarperBusiness, 1997.

Execution: The Discipline of Getting Things Done, by Larry Bossidy and Ron Charan. New York: Crown Business, 2002.

Good to Great: Why Some Companies Make the Leap … and Others Don't, by Jim Collins. New York: Harper-Collins, 2001.

The Five Temptations of a CEO: A Leadership Fable, by Patrick M. Lencioni. San Francisco: Jossey-Bass, 1998.

Jack: Straight from the Gut, by Jack Welch. New York: Warner, 2001.

The Goal: A Process of Ongoing Improvement (2nd edition),

by Eliyahu M. Goldratt. Great Barrington, Mass.: North River Press, 1992.

The One Minute Manager, by Kenneth Blanchard and Spencer Johnson. New York: William Morrow, 1982.

The Spirit to Serve: Marriott's Way, by J.W. Marriott Jr. New York: HarperCollins, 2001.

Who Says Elephants Can't Dance? Inside IBM's Historic Turnaround, by Louis V. Gerstner Jr. New York: HarperBusiness, 2002.

The Game of Work: How to Enjoy Work as Much as Play, by Charles A. Coonradt. Park City, Utah: Game of Work, 1997.

Managing the Obvious: How to Get What You Want Using What You Know, by Charles A. Coonradt, with Jack M. Lyons and Richard Williams. Park City, Utah: Game of Work, 1994.

Scorekeeping for Success, by Charles A. Coonradt. Park City, Utah: Game of Work, 1999.

Inspiration and Motivation

Chicken Soup for the Soul®, by Jack Canfield and Mark Victor Hansen. Deerfield Beach, Fla.: Health Communications, 1993.

Chicken Soup for the Soul at Work, by Jack Canfield, Mark Victor Hansen, Martin Rutte, Maida Rogerson, and Tim Clauss. Deerfield Beach, Fla.: Health Communications, 1996.

Chicken Soup for the Soul: Living Your Dreams, by Jack

Canfield and Mark Victor Hansen. Deerfield Beach, Fla.: Health Communications, 2003.

Dare to Win, by Jack Canfield and Mark Victor Hansen. New York: Berkley, 1994.

It's Not Over until You Win, by Les Brown. New York: Simon & Schuster, 1997.

Rudy's Rules for Success, by Rudy Ruettiger and Mike Celizic. Dallas, Tex.: Doddridge Press, 1995.

Health and Fitness

8 Minutes in the Morning, by Jorge Cruise. New York: HarperCollins, 2001.

The 24-Hour Turnaround: The Formula for Permanent Weight Loss, Antiaging, and Optimal Health—Starting Today! by Jay Williams, Ph.D. New York: Regan Books, 2002.

Body for Life: 12 Weeks to Mental and Spiritual Strength, by Bill Phillips. New York: HarperCollins, 1999.

The Mars and Venus Diet and Exercise Solution, by John Gray, Ph.D. New York: St. Martin's Press, 2003.

Stress Management Made Simple, by Jay Winner, M.D. Santa Barbara, Calif.: Blue Fountain Press, 2003.

Ultimate Fit or Fat, by Covert Bailey. Boston: Houghton Mifflin Company, 2000.

Time Management and Getting Things Done

First Things First, by Stephen Covey, A. Roger Merrill, and Rebecca R. Merrill. New York: Fireside, 1995.

Getting Things Done: The Art of Stress-Free Productivity, by David Allen. New York: Viking, 2001.

Getting Things Done, by Edwin C. Bliss. New York: Charles Scribner's Sons, 1991.

Doing It Now, by Edwin C. Bliss. New York: Macmillan, 1983.

The 10 Natural Laws of Successful Time and Life Management: Proven Strategies for Increased Productivity and Inner Peace, by Hyrum W. Smith. New York: Warner Books, 1994.

The Procrastinator's Handbook: Mastering the Art of Doing It Now, by Rita Emmett. New York: Walker Publishing, 2000.

Personal Awareness, Human Potential, Inner Peace and Spirituality

Loving What Is: Four Questions That Can Change Your Life, by Byron Katie. New York: Harmony Books, 2002.

The Sedona Method: Your Key to Lasting Happiness, Success, Peace and Emotional Well-being, by Hale Dwoskin. Sedona, Ariz.: Sedona Press, 2003.

The Four Agreements: A Practical Guide to Personal Freedom, by Don Miguel Ruiz. San Rafael: Amber-Allen, 1999.

The Power of Full Engagement, by Jim Loehr and Tony Schwartz. New York: Free Press, 2002.

Don't Sweat the Small Stuff … and It's All Small Stuff: Simple Ways to Keep the Little Things from Taking Over Your Life, by Richard Carlson. New York: Hyperion, 1997.

The Six Pillars of Self-Esteem, by Nathaniel Branden. New York: Bantam, 1994.

Life After Life, by Raymond A. Moody Jr., M.D. New York: Bantam, 1975.

Life Strategies: Doing What Works, Doing What Matters, by Phillip C. McGraw, Ph.D. New York: Hyperion, 1999.

Power vs. Force: The Hidden Determinants of Human Behavior, by David R. Hawkins, M.D., Ph.D. Carlsbad, Calif.: Hay House, 2002.

The Power of Now: A Guide to Spiritual Enlightenment, by Eckhart Tolle. Novato, Calif.: New World Library, 1999.

Eliminating Stress, Finding Inner Peace, by Brian Weiss, M.D. Carlsbad, Calif.: Hay House, 2003.

The Seven Spiritual Laws of Success, by Deepak Chopra. San Rafael, Calif.: Amber-Allen, 1994.

The Spirituality of Success: Getting Rich with Integrity, by Vincent M. Roazzi. Dallas: Brown Books, 2002.

The Way of the Spiritual Warrior (audio cassette), with David Gershon. Available from his Web site at www.empowermenttraining.com.

How to Say No Without Feeling Guilty: And Say Yes to More

Time and What Matters Most to You, by Patti Breitman and Connie Hatch. New York: Broadway, 2001.

When I Say No, I Feel Guilty, by Manuel J. Smith. New York: Bantam, 1975.

Coach Yourself to Success: 101 Tips from a Personal Coach for Reaching Your Goals at Work and in Life, by Talane Miedaner. Lincolnwood, Ill.: Contemporary Books, 2000.

Take Yourself to the Top: The Secrets of America's #1 Career Coach, by Laura Berman Fortgang. New York: Warner, 1998.

The Portable Coach: 28 Sure Fire Strategies for Business and Personal Success, by Thomas J. Leonard. New York: Scribner, 1998.

Developing Your Intuition

Divine Intuition: Your Guide to Creating a Life You Love, by Lynn A. Robinson. New York: Dorling Kindersley, 2001. Also check out Lynn's Web site at www.lynn-robinson.com.

PowerHunch, by Marcia Emery. Hillsboro, Ore.: Beyond Words Publishing, 2001.

Practical Intuition, by Laura Day. New York: Broadway Books, 1997.

Practical Intuition for Success, by Laura Day. New York: HarperCollins, 1997.

The Corporate Mystic, by Gay Hendricks and Kate Ludeman. New York: Bantam Books, 1997.

The Executive Mystic, by Barrie Dolnick. New York: HarperBusiness, 1999.

Audio Programs

The Success Principles: Your 30-Day Journey from Where You Are to Where You Want to Be, by Jack Canfield and Janet Switzer, is a 30-day course with 6 CDs and a 90-page workbook. It contains numerous worksheets and exercises to help you integrate the material presented here. You can also listen to the CDs in the car to reinforce your new learning. To order, go to www.thesuccessprinciples.com or www.jackcanfield.com or call +1-1-800-237-8336.

The following are the other motivational and educational audio programs I most recommend. All are available from Nightingale-Conant (www.nightingale.com) except one, which is indicated:

Action Strategies for Personal Achievement, by Brian Tracy
A View from the Top, by Zig Ziglar
The Aladdin Factor, by Jack Canfield and Mark Victor Hansen
The Art of Exceptional Living, by Jim Rohn
The Automatic Millionaire, by David Bach
Get the Edge, by Anthony Robbins
Goals, by Zig Ziglar
Guide to Everyday Negotiating, by Roger Dawson
Jump and the Net Will Appear, by Robin Crow

Live with Passion, by Anthony Robbins

Magical Mind, Magical Body, by Deepak Chopra

Maximum Confidence, by Jack Canfield

Multiple Streams of Income, by Robert Allen

The New Dynamics of Winning, by Denis Waitley

The New Psycho-Cybernetics, by Maxwell Maltz and Dan Kennedy

The One Minute Millionaire System, by Mark Victor Hansen and Robert Allen

The Power of Purpose, by Les Brown

The Power of Visualization, by Dr. Lee Pulos

The Psychology of Achievement, by Brian Tracy

The Psychology of Selling, by Brian Tracy

Pure Genius, by Dan Sullivan

Rich Dad Secrets, by Robert Kiyosaki

The Secrets to Manifesting Your Destiny, by Wayne Dyer

The 7 Habits of Highly Effective People, by Stephen Covey

Self-Esteem and Peak Performance, by Jack Canfield (CareerTrack)

The Weekend Millionaire's Real Estate Investing Program, by Roger Dawson and Mike Summey

Think and Grow Rich, by Napoleon Hill

Human Potential and Self-Development Training

Canfield Training Group, P.O. Box 30880, Santa Barbara, CA 93130, USA. Phone: +1-805-563-2935. Fax: +1-805-563-2945. www.jackcanfield.com. Throughout the year, I conduct day-long, weekend, and week-long training programs that focus on Living the Success Principles, Living Your Highest Vision, the Power of Focus, Self-Esteem and Peak Performance, Maximum Confidence, and the Training of Trainers Program.

Global Relationship Centers, 25555 Pedernales Point Drive, Spicewood, TX 78669, USA. Phone: +1-512-264-3333. Fax: +1-512-264-2913. www.grc333.com. Larry Price, the executive director of my foundation – the Foundation for Self-Esteem – took their Understanding Yourself and Others program and received tremendous value from it.

The Hendricks Institute, 402 W. Ojai Avenue, Suite 101, PMB 413, Ojai, CA 93023, USA. Phone: +1-800-688-0772. www.hendricks.com. Gay and Katie Hendricks offer a variety of courses, both live and online, on relationships and conscious living. My wife and I have both benefited deeply from their work.

Hoffman Institute, 223 San Anselmo Avenue, Suite 4, San Anselmo, CA 94960, USA. Phone: +1-415-485-5220. www.hoffmaninstitute.org. This powerful week-long training helps you make peace with your parents and

overcome the limiting beliefs and reactive behavior
patterns that you developed as a child. My partner Mark
Victor Hansen recently took it, as did Martin Rutte and
Tim Claus, coauthors of *Chicken Soup for the Soul at
Work*. My son Oran, now 30, also took it, and it radical-
ly changed his life.

Human Awareness Institute. Phone: +1-650-571-5524.
www.hai.org. Offers workshops on opening the heart,
creating intimate relationships, and for individuals and
couples. The institute has offices in Australia and the
United Kingdom, as well as throughout the United
States.

Insight Seminars, 2101 Wilshire Boulevard, Suite 101, Santa Monica, CA 90403, USA. Phone: +1-310-315-9733.
Fax: +1-310-315-9854. www.insightseminars.org. A single weekend seminar provides an opportunity to transform your life, experience a deeper connection with
your true self, and create greater balance and personal
fulfillment. The advanced courses assist you in letting
go of fears and limiting behaviors, cultivate greater ability to access your wisdom, intuition, and inner mag-
nificence, and live your life in greater alignment with
your spiritual values.

Landmark Education – The Forum, 353 Sacramento Street,
Suite 200, San Francisco, CA 94111, USA. Phone: +1-
415-981-8850. Fax: +1-415-616-2411. www.landmark-
education.com. This powerful weekend training takes
you out of fear into living a dynamic, intentional life of
contribution and fulfillment. You can expect greater

self-esteem, more fulfilling relationships, greater financial success, and more balance in your life.

Money and You Program of the Excellerated Business School for Entrepreneurs, 4878 Pescadero Avenue, Suite 204, San Diego, CA 92107, USA. Phone: +1-619-224-8880. www.excellerated.com. Conducts breakthrough, transformational workshops on money and business for entrepreneurs.

Peak Potentials Training, 1651 Welch Street, North Vancouver, BC, Canada, V7P 3G9. Phone: +1-604-983-3344. www.peakpotentials.com. I strongly recommend Harv Eker's Millionaire Mind weekend. It is his core training. Sign up for a free Millionaire Mind Evening Teleseminar on the Web site to get more information. There are also many graduate seminars you can take on a variety of topics, including a powerful training-of-trainers course.

PSI Seminars, 11650 High Valley Road, Clearlake Oaks, CA 95423, USA. Phone: +1-707-998-2222. www.psi-seminars.com. The company offers a series of powerful transformational seminars.

Sedona Training Associates, 60 Tortilla Drive, Sedona, AZ 86336, USA. Phone: +1-928-282-3522. Fax: +1-928-203-0602. www.sedona.com. The Sedona Method is one of the easiest and most powerful tools for self-improvement and spiritual growth that I have ever experienced. I have been amazed at the simplicity of the method and the powerful effect it has had on my life. It focuses on releasing emotions so that you come back into touch with the deepest part of your nature. Life gets easier. There is less resistance to everything. It helps you release anxiety and fears, eliminate stress, manage anger, overcome depression, improve relationships, enjoy more energy, sleep more soundly, achieve more radiant health, and find lasting inner peace, joy, and love.

The Breakthrough Experience with Dr. John Demartini, Demartini Seminars, 2800 Post Oak Boulevard, Suite 5250, Houston, TX 77056, USA. Phone: +1-713-850-1234. www.drdemartini.com. John is a master facilitator and a truly wise and profound being.

Coaching Programs

For information on The Success Principles Coaching Program, which is designed to personally help you integrate these principles into your life, career, relationship, and finances, visit www.thesuccessprinciples.com/coaching.htm or www.jackcanfield.com

These are my other two favorite coaching programs:

The Strategic Coach Program was created by Dan Sullivan. Contact the organization at +1-416-531-7399, or visit www.strategiccoach.com. Dan also has a host of books, audios, and other media based on core Strategic Coach concepts and tools.

Achievers Coaching Program was created by Les Hewitt (who coauthored *The Power of Focus* with Mark Victor

Hansen and me) and has offices in four countries. Contact the organization by writing Achievers Canada, suite 220, 2421 37th Avenue, Calgary, Alberta T2E 6Y7, Canada; calling +1-403-295-0500; or visiting www.the-poweroffocus.ca.

To find a personal coach, contact
The International Coach Federation.
   Visit: www.coachfederation.org.
Coach U. Visit www.coachinc.com. Click on Find a Coach.
Other coaches – especially those that specialize in a specific industry or business how-to training – have Web sites that can be found with a simple Internet search like "real estate coaching." One of the best in that category, by the way, is Mike Ferry's Real Estate Coaching at www.mikeferry.com.

Additional Resources

The ededge book club, is a powerful way to stay on the cutting edge of breakthrough business success books. To enroll in the service, go to www.positivedeviantnetwork.com.

   Chicken Soup's Daily Serving (www.chickensoup.com) is a free daily e-mail of a heartwarming, inspirational story from the best-selling *Chicken Soup for the Soul*® series.

About the Authors

Jack Canfield has been a successful author, professional speaker, seminar leader, corporate trainer, and entrepreneur. After graduating from Harvard University, Jack started his career as a high school teacher in Chicago's inner city. Jack quickly became obsessed with learning how to motivate his unmotivated students. In this quest, he discovered self-made Chicago millionaire and success guru W. Clement Stone. Stone was the publisher of *Success Magazine*, the president of Combined Insurance Corporation, the author of *The Success System That Never Fails*, and coauthor, with Napoleon Hill, of *Success Through a Positive Mental Attitude*.

Jack went to work at the W. Clement & Jessie V. Stone Foundation with the charge to take these success principles into the schools and Boys Clubs of the greater Chicago area – and later the entire Midwest. Wanting to understand these achievement motivation principles even more clearly, Jack returned to graduate school at the University of Massachusetts, where he received his master's degree in psychological education. After graduating, Jack embarked on a career of conducting seminars for schoolteachers, counselors, psychotherapists, and – later – corporate leaders, managers, salespeople, and entrepreneurs, teaching the principles of self-esteem, peak performance, achievement motivation, and success.

Along the way, Jack wrote and coauthored such books as *100 Ways to Enhance Self-Esteem in the Classroom*, *Dare to Win*, *The Aladdin Factor*, *Heart at Work*, and *The Power of Focus: How to Hit All Your Personal, Business and Financial Goals with Absolute Certainty*, as well as the best-selling 105-book *Chicken Soup for the Soul®* series, which has currently sold over 100 million copies in 46 languages around the world. Jack has also shared his principles for success, self-esteem, and happiness in his best-selling CareerTrack audio album *Self-Esteem and Peak Performance* and his Nightingale-Conant albums *Maximum Confidence* and *The Aladdin Factor*.

Because he's in demand more days each year than he could possibly speak and do seminars, Jack has also created two video-based training programs: the STAR Program, which is his basic self-esteem and peak performance training for corporations and schools, and the GOALS Program, which are the same principles presented for at-risk populations such as welfare recipients and prisoners.

Organizations and corporations that have sought Jack out to share these principles with their members and employees include Virgin Records, Sony Pictures, Merrill Lynch, Monsanto, ITT Hartford Insurance, GlaxoSmithKline, Scott Paper, The Million Dollar Forum, Coldwell Banker, RE/MAX, FedEx, Campbell's Soup, TRW, Society of Real Estate Professionals, the Million Dollar Round-table, American Society of Training & Development, Ameritech, NCR, Young Presidents' Organization, Chief Executives Organization, GE, Income Builders International, U.S. Department of the Navy, Siemens, Cingular Wireless, Southern Bell, Domino's Pizza, Accenture, Bergen Brunswig Pharmaceuticals, Children's Miracle Network, UCLA, University of Michigan, the Council for Excellence in Government, and hundreds of others.

Jack has given speeches and conducted workshops in all 50 states in the United States, as well as in Canada, Mexico, Europe, Asia, Africa, and Australia. He has also appeared on over 600 radio shows and 200 television shows, including *Larry King Live, 20/20, Inside Edition,* the *Today* show, *Oprah, Fox and Friends, CBS Evening News, NBC Nightly News, Eye to Eye,* and *CNN's Talk Back Live!* and on PBS and QVC.

Jack conducts one-day and weekend workshops that focus on Living the Success Principles, the Power of Focus, Self-Esteem and Peak Performance, and Maximum Confidence, as well as an annual 7-day Breakthrough to Success: Living the Success Principles training in which he teaches the principles of success in a powerful, life-changing workshop. His trainings are designed for businesspeople, managers, entrepreneurs, salespeople, sales managers, managers, educators, counselors, coaches, consultants, ministers, and others who are interested in maximizing their personal and professional success.

To find out more about Jack's workshops and training,

books, and audio and video training programs or to inquire about Jack's availability as a speaker or trainer, you can contact his office at

The Jack Canfield Companies
P.O. Box 30880, Santa Barbara, CA 93130, USA

Phones: +1-805-563-2935 and
+1-800-237-8336; fax: +1-805-563-2945
Web site: www.jackcanfield.com

Janet Switzer, from her first job as campaign coordinator for a member of Congress at age 19 to building an international publishing company with over $10 million in assets by age 29, epitomizes the personal achievement and professional accomplishment that comes from applying these proven principles of success.

Today, she's the marketing genius and business growth expert of choice for some of the world's top success gurus: peak performance expert Jack Canfield, master motivator Mark Victor Hansen, marketing icon Jay Abraham, Internet income expert Yanik Silver, and *Jesus CEO* author Laurie Beth Jones, among others. Additionally, Janet has counseled more than 50,000 companies and entrepreneurs worldwide in leveraging their intangibles and information assets for untold millions in potential windfall revenue. She's the author of the Instant Income® series of small-business marketing resources designed to help entrepreneurs not only create immediate cash flow for their business but develop lucrative new profit centers, too. For details, visit www.instantincome.com.

Janet is an internationally recognized keynote speaker and founder and editor of *Leading Experts* magazine – as well as a columnist with *Training Magazine Asia* and numerous newswires and press syndicates.

She regularly speaks to thousands of entrepreneurs, independent sales professionals, corporate employees, and industry association members on the principles of success and income generation. Additionally, she helps achievers who are experts in their field attain worldwide status and million-dollar incomes by building publishing empires around their business strategies, training concepts, industry expertise, and unique market posture. Her multimedia short course "How Experts Build Empires: The Step-By-Step System for Turning Your Expertise into Super-Lucrative Profit Centers" is the industry's definitive work on the subject of developing and marketing information products.

Janet makes her home in Thousand Oaks, California, where she belongs to Calvary Community Church and works with young people as a local 4-H Club project leader – a role she's enjoyed for nearly 20 years.

To bring Janet to your next event, call +1-805-499-9400 or visit www.janetswitzer.com. To subscribe to *Leading Experts e-Magazine*, visit www.leadingexperts.net.

Permissions

We acknowledge the many publishers and individuals who granted us permission to reprint the cited material:

© Randy Glasbergen, www.glasbergen.com.

Charles Rodrigues © 1991 Tribune Media Services. Reprinted with permission.

D.C. Cordova. Reprinted with permission.

T. Harv Eker, interviewed by author.

Anthony Robbins. Reprinted with permission.

Monty Roberts, interviewed by author.

Julie Laipply, interviewed by author.

Pat Williams, interviewed by author.

Arnold M. Patent. Reprinted with permission.

© Randy Glasbergen, www.glasbergen.com.

Dave Liniger, interviewed by author.

Adapted from "Placebos Prove So Powerful Even Experts Are Surprised: New Studies Explore the Brain's Triumph Over Reality" by Sandra Blakeslee, *New York Times*, October 13, 1998, section F, page 1. Reprinted with permission.

Timothy Ferriss, interviewed by author.

Ruben Gonzalez, interviewed by author.

Stephen J. Cannell, interviewed by author.

Peak Performers, by Charles A. Garfield, Ph.D. Reprinted with permission.

Buddy Hickerson. © Tribune Media Services. Reprinted with permission. Daniel Amen, M.D., director of Amen Clinics, Inc. and author of *Change Your Brain, Change Your Life*.

Stan Dale, D.H.S. Reprinted with permission.

Captain Gerald Coffee. Reprinted with permission.

Reprinted with special permission of King Features Syndicate.

Stuart Lichtman, interviewed by author.

Brian Tracy. Reprinted with permission.

Les Hewitt. Reprinted with permission.

Copyright © 1994 Stephen Rebello. Originally published in *Movieline*, July 1994. All rights reserved. Reprinted by arrangement with Mary Evans, Inc. © 1998 The New Yorker Collection. William Haefeli from cartoonbank.com. All rights reserved.

Peter Vidmar. Reprinted with permission.

John Assaraf, interviewed by author.

Marilyn Kentz, interviewed by author.

Caryl Kristensen. Reprinted with permission.

Diana von Welanetz Wentworth. Reprinted with permission.

www.cartoonstock.com. Reprinted with permission. Jack Bierman. Reprinted with permission.

© 1990 Thaves. Reprinted with permission. Newspaper distributed by NEA, Inc.

Jeff Arch, interviewed by author.

Michael T. Kelley, interviewed by author.

Dr. John Demartini, interviewed by author.

Richard Paul Evans. Reprinted with permission.

Robert Allen, interviewed by author.

Sylvia Collins. Reprinted with permission.

Dale and Donna Hutcherson. Reprinted with permission.

Chad Pregracke. Reprinted with permission.

Debbie Macomber, *New York Times* best-selling author. Reprinted with permission.

Jaroldeen Edwards. Reprinted with permission.

Martin Rutte is at www.martinrutte.com. Reprinted with permission.

Take your success to the next level …

Download The Success Principles FREE Success Tools™
at: www.thesuccessprinciples.com/tools.html

FREE One-Year Planning Guide? to help you plan your activities, to-do list, action items, success reading, Breakthrough Results time-management schedule, and more. Includes page after page of colorful daily checklists, notes pages, goal-setting pages, reading lists, personal journal entries, inspirational and thought-provoking messages from Jack and Janet … and more.

FREE Victory Log … for your three-ring binder or other victory log format. These letter-size pages are colorful, inspiring, and designed to empower you with daily successes you create. When times are tough, remind yourself how successful you really are – with your own Victory Log pages designed to coordinate with The Success Principles Audio Program.

FREE Mastermind Strategy Guide … designed specifically for mastermind groups, this free strategy guide helps your group with activities, ideas, and thought-provoking messages that can help any group break through to a higher level of success!

The Success Principles
Annual Success Challenge™

Every year, Janet and I select individuals from more than a dozen categories who demonstrate a significant increase in their personal or professional success. Perhaps you've overcome a substantial obstacle … discovered a new purpose … pursued a new path.

You could win The Success Challenge when you read and apply The Success Principles to your life. Find out how by visiting www.thesuccessprinciples.com!

The Success Principles
Free success strategies course™

In this powerful, FREE online course – delivered to your e-mail address – you'll discover easy-to-use strategies that will help you decide what you want … and get it. Register today at www.thesuccessprinciples.com.

Index

Achievers Focusing System 103
affirmations 110, 116–24, 195, 296
age 67, 68–9
alcohol 7, 13
Alcoholics Anonymous 13
Allen, Robert 190–5
Amen, Dr. Daniel 68–9
Arch, Jeff 173–5
asking
    and comfort zones 204
    fear of 198–9
    for feedback 226–33
    and lists 208
    power of 206–7
    and rejection 217
    and risks 205–6
    techniques 200–3
Assaraf, John 138–9, 263–5

Bassett, Peggy 77–8
Bell, Alexander Graham 217–18
Bierman, Jack 163–4
blame 2–7, 14–17, 230, 266, 267
Blanchard, Ken 256, 291

Booth, Rev. Leo 291
Borgnine, Ernest 302
Boxer, Barbara 7
Bragg, Dr. Paul 186–7
brain research 53–4, 61, 127–8, 131, 141
Brause, Diane 43
Brin, Sergei 218
Brockovich, Erin 7

Callahan, Dr. Roger 182
Cannell, Stephen J. 62–3
careers
    and breakthrough goals 82–4
    ideal 43–4, 50
    and self-belief 62–3
Carrey, Jim 89–90
Carter-Scott, Chérie 41–2
charitable work 47, 51
Cheney, Dick 68
Clark, General Wesley 46
Clinton, Bill 196
Cobb, Ty 67
Coffee, Captain Jerry 73–4

Collins, Sylvia 203–4
comfort zones 109–116, 172, 204
complaining *see* blame
completion 270–8, 296
conditioned responses 8, 53–7
Cordova, D. C., 105
core genius 285–91
Cortez, Hernando 174–5
Couples, Fred 143–4
Creasey, John 219

Dagett, Tim 132–6
DeAngelis, Barbara 256
DeGeneres, Ellen 43
delegation 286–8, 289–90
Demartini, Dr. John 186–8
desires
    defining 37, 40–3
    other peoples' 39–40
Di Bona, Vin 301
Domingo, Placido 197
Durning, Charles 302

education 67–8
    and breakthrough goals 83
Edwards, Carolyn 259–60
Edwards, Jaroldeen 259–60
Eker, Harv 105
Eller, Karl 196
Eller, Stevie 196–7
Ellison, Larry 67
Evans, Richard Paul 189–90
Everhart, Angie 218
exercises
    Life Purpose 35–6
    The Vision Exercise 49–52

expectations
    conditioning 53–7
    negative 63–4
    positive 53–7, 70–7, 89

fear
    disappearing 177–9
    facing 180–1, 295
    and feedback 293–4
    and imagination 175–7
    and incompletes 271
    phobias 182–3
    and risks 173–5, 181, 184–95
feedback 24–5, 155, 161–4
    asking for 226–33
    and failure 236–8
    listening to 234
    patterns in 235–6
    responding to 222–6
    types of 220–1
Feinstein, Dianne 7
Ferris, Tim 56–7, 261
Five-Minute Phobia Cure 182–3
Ford, Harrison 257
Fox, Terry 248
Frost, David 252
Fuller, Buckminster 46, 298, 303

Garfield, Dr. Charles 65–6
Garr, Teri 302
Gates, Bill 7, 46, 67–8
Giuliani, Rudolf 197
Gonzalez, Ruben 58–9, 158–60,
    302–3
goals
    acting "as if" 141–53

breakthrough 82–4, 86–7, 96, 99
chunk it down 97–103
and feedback 221–4
Goals Book 86, 88, 139–40
and improvement 241
mastery 95
measurable 80
obstacles to success 90–3
positive statement of 79–80
reviewing 84–5
setting 87–90
taking action 292–7
writing down 81, 96, 130
see also vizualization
Gray, John 105, 256

habits 7, 279–84, 286, 296–7
Hamilton, Scott 158
Hammerstein, Oscar 251
Hansen, Mark Victor 47, 76–7, 84, 86, 137, 200, 211, 213–14, 256, 291, 294, 299, 300–1
health
and responsibility 2
The Vision Exercise 50
weight-loss 232–3
Hendricks, Gay 105
Hendricks, Kathlyn 105
Herman, Jeff 213
Hewitt, Les 103
Hill, Napoleon 3, 53
Holtz, Lou 87–8
Hutcherson, Dale 205–6
Hutcherson, Donna 205

improvement 239–45
Ito, Judge Lance 258

Jamal, Azim 140
Jeffers, Susan 148, 172, 291
Jenner, Bruce, 85
Jesus Christ 95
Jobs, Steve 7

Kelley, Mike 184–5
Kennedy, John F. 46, 131
Kentz, Marilyn 139–40, 151
kinesiology 63–4
King, Martin Luther Jr. 46
King, Stephen 218
Kremer, John 256
Kriegel, Otis 161
Kristensen, Caryl 139–40, 151
Kroc, Ray 166

Laipply, Julie 31–2
Lee, Bruce 88–9
Lemmon, Jack 302
Lichtman, Stu 91–2
Liniger, Dave 46, 299
Little, Rick 215
Lucas, George 197

McCain 197
McCartney, Paul 257
McGraw, Tug 55–6
Macomber, Debbie 249–51
Macomber, Wayne 249–50
meditation 36, 130, 140
Miedaner, Talane 277
Millman, Dan 291

mind mapping 98–101
money
    and responsibility 2
    The Vision Exercise 49
Muhammad Ali 166

Nantz, Jim 143–4
Nicklaus, Jack 126

O'Brien, Dan 85
O'Dell, Tawni 251–2
opportunities 70–7
Orfalea, Paul 299–300
Orton, Carl 217–18

Page, Larry 218
Panero, Hugh 246–7
Peary, Robert 251
Peck, Scott 256
Peres, Shimon 197
Perot, H. Ross 252
persistence
    and obstacles 245–6, 251–5
    and sacrifice 249–51
    short-term goals 247
personal responsibility 1–27,
        303–4
    and self-belief 61
Piazza, Dr. Ignatius 216–17
Poitier, Sidney 7, 257
Poynter, Dan 256
precessional effects 298–303
Pregracke, Chad 206–7
purpose
    discovering 28, 31–4
    Exercise 35–6

statements of 29–30
quantum physics 102

Ramirez, Mary Alice 207
recreation 50
rejection
    dealing with 209–11
    and perseverance 211–15
    well-known examples 217–19
relationships
    and feedback 228–9
    improving 105
    and responsibility 2, 20
    The Vision Exercise 50
Resnick, Dr. Robert 6
responses
    changing 12–13, 22
    and outcomes 6, 10–11
risks 17–18, 173–5, 181, 184–95,
        205–6
Robbins, Anthony 181, 289,
        291
Roberts, Monty 48
Robinson, Jackie 7
Rohn, Jim 261
Rosenblum, Jack 235
Rule of five 256–60
Rutte, Martin 274

Sakamoto, Makoto 134
Sanders, Col. Harlan 212
Satir, Virginia 233
Schwartz, David 88
Scolastico, Ron 257
Seidler 214
self-belief

and focus 62–3
and negative expectations
    63–4
and positive expectations
    54–9, 62–3
success in sport 55–9, 62, 85
throwing off the past 61
Sheen, Martin 302
Shinn, Florence Scovell 122
Shultz, Laura 65–6
smoking 7
Sosa, Sammy 289
Spielberg, Stephen 257
Stallone, Sylvester 166
Starwoman, Athena 186
Stehling, Wendy 232–3
Steiger, Rod 302
Stone, W. Clement 3, 70, 72, 86,
    122, 166, 266–7
Streisand, Barbara 257
success
    and action 154–70, 292–8
    and big dreams 46–8, 94
    clues 104–7
    and core genius 285–91
    and desire 43, 45
    and failure 167–70
    learning from others 263–9
    obstacles to 90–3
    and positive expectations
        70–7
    and purpose 29
    and rejection 211–19
    releasing the brakes 108–24
    and responsibility 1, 2–4, 23
    and risks 183–5, 205–6

and self-belief 53–9
and stopping complaining 19
to-do lists 102–3
see also asking; goals;
    rejection; visualization
Sullivan, Dan 288

Tabler, Pat 253–4
Tarcher, Carl 299
Thurber, Marshall 105
Tracy, Brian 101
True, Herbert 203
Trump, Donald 43, 299
Tutu, Desmond 197

Vegso, Peter 214
Vidmar, Peter 132–6
visualization 57, 102, 120–4, 296
    and the brain 125–8
    process of 129–32
    in sport 126, 132–6
    techniques 136–40

Washington, Denzel 7, 152
Weaver, Dennis 291
Weintraub, Lloyd 301
Welanetz Wentworth, Diana
    von 146, 290–1, 300–1
Wepner, Chuck 166
Williams, Pat 33–4
Winfrey, Oprah 43, 82, 148, 25?
Woods, Tiger 43, 288–9

yellow alerts 21–3

Zimbalist, Stephanie 302